James Sutherland Cotton

Mountstuart Elphinstone, and the Making of Southwestern India

James Sutherland Cotton

Mountstuart Elphinstone, and the Making of Southwestern India

ISBN/EAN: 9783337289362

Printed in Europe, USA, Canada, Australia, Japan

Cover: Foto ©ninafisch / pixelio.de

More available books at **www.hansebooks.com**

Mountstuart Elphinstone

AND THE
MAKING OF SOUTH-WESTERN INDIA

By J. S. COTTON, M.A.

THIRD THOUSAND

Oxford
AT THE CLARENDON PRESS: 1896

HUNC LIBELLUM

IN QUO VIRI EGREGII

ACTORIS EIUSDEMQUE SCRIPTORIS

RERUM APUD INDOS GESTARUM

VITA MORESQUE CONTINENTUR

FILIOLAE SUAE

PIETATIS IN PATREM

NECNON OPERAE IMPENSAE MEMOR

D. D. D.

J. S. C.

A. D. VIII ID. FEB. MDCCCXCII.

PREFACE

MATERIALS for the life of Mountstuart Elphinstone are abundant. In 1861, two years after his death, Sir T. E. Colebrooke, Bart., who had known him intimately during his later years, contributed an obituary of exceptional length and authority to the *Journal* of the Royal Asiatic Society (Old Series, xxviii, 221 sq.). The whole of his voluminous papers—journals, letters, despatches, and minutes—were afterwards entrusted to Sir T. E. Colebrooke, for the purpose of writing a formal biography, which was published in 1884, in two volumes, illustrated with portraits and maps. These form the basis of the present sketch; and from them all the quotations, unless otherwise specified, have been taken. In the same year (1884) appeared a volume of "Selections from the Minutes and other Official Writings of Mountstuart Elphinstone," edited by Prof. George W. Forrest, with an introductory memoir. Much use also has been made of this volume, though the dates of the documents given in it often require to be corrected from other sources. Finally, Sir J. W. Kaye's Memoir, in his "Lives of Indian Officers" (new edition, 1890), contains some information, both personal and documentary, not to be found elsewhere.

The engraving that forms the frontispiece has been kindly lent by Mr. John Murray.

CONTENTS

CHAP.		PAGES
I.	INTRODUCTION	9–16
II.	EARLY LIFE: ARRIVAL IN INDIA	17–21
III.	FIRST APPOINTMENT TO POONA	22–30
IV.	THE SECOND MARÁTHÁ WAR	31–44
V.	NÁGPUR, AND SINDIA'S CAMP	45–58
VI.	THE KÁBUL MISSION	59–74
VII.	RESIDENT AT POONA	75–100
VIII.	THE THIRD MARÁTHÁ WAR	101–120
IX.	THE SETTLEMENT OF THE DECCAN	121–158
X.	GOVERNOR OF BOMBAY	159–200
XI.	RETURN HOME: RETIREMENT IN ENGLAND	201–217
	INDEX	219–222

NOTE

The orthography of proper names follows the system adopted by the Indian Government for the *Imperial Gazetteer of India*. That system, while adhering to the popular spelling of very well-known places, such as Punjab, Poona, Deccan, etc., employs in all other cases the vowels with the following uniform sounds :—

a, as in woman : *á*, as in land : *i*, as in police : *í*, as in intrigue : *o*, as in cold : *u*, as in bull : *ú*, as in rule.

MOUNTSTUART ELPHINSTONE

CHAPTER I

INTRODUCTION

ON the long roll of civil servants of the East India Company, no name possesses a greater charm than that of Mountstuart Elphinstone. As diplomatist and administrator, he exercised a decisive influence upon the fate of Western India, at the critical epoch when British order had to be substituted for Maráthá turbulence: his memory is still revered in Bombay —by English and natives alike—for nobility of character, justice, and encouragement of education: his *History of India* has won for him a permanent place in literature. Elphinstone's long life witnessed almost the entire drama of British conquest. Born in 1779, when Warren Hastings was still Governor-General, he went out to India in 1796, before Tipu had been finally subdued. In 1803, he rode by the side of the future Duke of Wellington at his first great victory. At the maturity of his powers he foiled the intrigues of the Peshwa, defeated him in battle, and annexed his dominions.

To him the Bombay Presidency owes both the enlargement of its territory and the organisation of its administrative system. Returning home after more than thirty years of uninterrupted labour, he passed his remaining days in retirement, venerated and consulted as the Nestor of the service. He died in 1859, having survived the Mutiny and the transfer of the government from the Company to the Crown.

The name of Elphinstone, therefore, has been chosen to head the volume in the series of Rulers of India which will tell the story of the overthrow of Maráthá supremacy and the introduction of British rule into the Deccan. But the exigencies of biographical treatment must not be allowed to hide the fact that Elphinstone was merely one among a devoted band of Company's servants, who, at the beginning of the present century, carried into execution the policy designed by the master-mind of the Marquis Wellesley; just as, fifty years later, a similar group of illustrious men gathered round Dalhousie and drew their inspiration from his genius. Some of those of the elder generation—such as Barry Close, Webbe, Jenkins, and Adam—can scarcely be said to emerge from the mists that condemn to obscurity all but the most fortunate of Anglo-Indian worthies. Three, however, of Elphinstone's contemporaries stand conspicuous for work of the same kind as that accomplished by himself; nor has history been careful to discriminate the merits of Charles Lord Metcalfe, Sir John Malcolm, Sir Thomas Munro, and the special subject of this little book. To name any one of them is to call up before the mind the other three. For their careers touched at many points; and it must always be remembered to their honour that none of them ever allowed ambition to interfere with their mutual friendship, or to impair the high opinion which they alike entertained of one another's abilities.

The beginning of the century was, indeed, the golden age of the Company's service. Clive and Hastings had shown to what rank the humblest 'writer' might attain; the cancer of corruption had been extirpated, and commercial duties had been thrust into the background. The Governor-Generals, being henceforth taken from the ranks of English statesmen, were largely dependent upon subordinates acquainted with the character and languages of the natives. Closer relations with the 'country powers' called into existence a new class of diplomatists, destined to be famous under the style of Residents; while frequent hostilities taught them their business in the most practical fashion. Outside Bengal and the Karnatik, almost all India was practically unexplored territory. British supremacy, even in arms, was far from being universally recognised. None could say what disaster might not result from an alliance between Tipu and the Nizam, or from an attack by the combined forces of the Marátha Chiefs. Above all, a constant fear occupied the minds of the English

in India, lest Napoleon should at any time follow in
the steps of Alexander, and transfer his genius for
war to the Far East.

Amid such stimulating conditions English and
Scotch boys were launched into active life at an age
when they would now be still at school. Malcolm—
who never ceased to be boyish in his pleasures—
obtained a cadetship at the age of twelve and landed
at Madras before he was fourteen; Metcalfe, who happened
to have been born at Calcutta, returned thither
as a 'writer' at fifteen; Elphinstone also left home
at fifteen; Munro at eighteen. Nor was it long ere
each of these youngsters found responsible employment.
Elphinstone was only twenty-four when he was
appointed Resident at Nágpur at a critical period of
affairs, and not yet thirty when sent on an embassy
to the court of Kábul. Unhampered by the telegraph,
or even by regular posts, the young diplomatists
were compelled to rely on their own resources, and
often to decide without instructions upon measures
of supreme importance. The sense of responsibility,
thus early developed, served them in good stead when
emergencies arrived. A conspicuous example is
afforded by Elphinstone's conduct before the battle of
Kirkí. He knew well that the Peshwa was trying
to deceive him—that he was collecting an immense
force to overwhelm the small British garrison; that
he was tampering with the loyalty of the Sepoys;
that he was even plotting his own assassination—yet
he never swerved from his policy of postponing the

crisis as long as possible, in order to avoid interference with the plans of the Governor-General; and he lived his usual life in the Residency, almost at the mercy of the enemy, until the very morning of the outbreak.

Another characteristic which marks this generation of Anglo-Indians was the union of bodily activity with intellectual accomplishments. In their long journeys from court to court, or when accompanying troops on the march, they lived an open-air life, and were equally at home in the camp, the hunting-field, and the Darbár. Malcolm, whose superb physique was the admiration of the others, is still remembered as a mighty Nimrod. He is related to have broken up a diplomatic conference on the news of the near neighbourhood of a tiger. From Malcolm's example his young assistant Outram learned how to pacify Central India by taming the savage tribe of Bhíls, and exterminating the wild beasts. Of Elphinstone it is not recorded that he was ever successful in his attempts to kill a tiger; but he was devoted to the Oriental sport of hawking and the English sport of 'pig-sticking.' Of all these men it may be said that, if their destiny had not made them diplomatists and administrators, they were capable of winning fame in war. Malcolm and Munro were both soldiers by profession, though their reputation does not rest upon their military exploits. Yet Malcolm probably never enjoyed a happier hour than when leading his brigade into action at Mehidpur; while Munro's achievement in subjugating the Southern Marátha country, with less than a complete battalion, earned a warm panegyric from Canning in the House of Commons. Wellington said of Elphinstone, after he had beheld his behaviour under fire at Assaye and Argáum, that he had mistaken his vocation and ought to have been a soldier. Metcalfe similarly conciliated the goodwill of the rugged veteran Lord Lake, who had at first despised him as a boy-civilian, by joining the storming party at Díg.

The men of that time enjoyed yet another advantage, which their successors perhaps envy them most of all. They did not work under the constant high pressure which now impairs the energies of Indian officials. Months could then be taken for journeys that are now done in as many days. Elphinstone spent two months in going up country to his first appointment at Benares, and something like eleven months in wandering across the peninsula on his devious way from Calcutta to Poona. When once settled, nothing could be more different from their ordinary placid life than the modern whirl of despatch-boxes and reports. Interrogatories by telegraph, newspaper criticism, questions in Parliament, visits from holiday tourists, were to them alike unknown. And the leisure thus allowed was in many cases put to excellent use. That these men wrote easily and well was but a necessary condition of their official duties. The same may be said of their familiar acquaintance with the vernacular languages. But when we consider the paltry stock of knowledge they must have taken out with them as boys, their subsequent devotion to learning becomes a marvel. The record of Elphinstone's reading during the eleven months' journey referred to above (when he was only twenty-one years of age) would not discredit Macaulay[1]. A week after the battle of Assaye he wrote to a friend: 'I am reading all Shakspere critically ... I have borrowed a capital Shakspere for reading. It has not one note, and I have (in consequence) never met with a difficulty.' At a later period he used to travel with two camel-loads of books, so packed that he could lay his hand on any volume he wished. Elphinstone's *History of India*, Malcolm's *History of Persia*, and Grant Duff's *History of the Maráthás*, are but a few examples of the many contributions made to literature about this time by Indian officials.

And, finally, it is pleasant to add that this group of public servants not only rose to the highest places which India affords, but also won recognition at home. Elphinstone was selected from among the rest by the Court of Directors to be Governor of Bombay at the early age of 39. After his retirement he more than once refused the Governor-Generalship, which no servant of the Company held between Lord Teignmouth and Lord Lawrence. Metcalfe was deprived, through the exigencies of party needs, of the rank of Governor-General, though he performed the

[1] See *post* (pp. 27, 28).

duties for twelve months. But he was twice chosen by the Ministers of the Crown to govern a great colony, each time at a crisis of its affairs, and was ultimately rewarded with a peerage. Malcolm received, to his own great delight, the first broad ribbon of the Bath ever given to an Anglo-Indian for civilian services, and succeeded Elphinstone at Bombay. Munro became Governor of Madras, K.C.B., and a baronet.

Such were the foremost of that band of men, trained in the school of Wellesley, who each contributed his share to the work of crushing the Maráthá confederation, and making the power of the British supreme throughout India.

CHAPTER II

EARLY LIFE: ARRIVAL IN INDIA

1779—1799

THE Honourable Mountstuart Elphinstone was born on the 6th October, 1779. Concerning the place of his birth his painstaking biographer has been unable to find a record, though there seems no doubt of the date. In his own diary at Haidarábád, in the year 1801, it is found written: 'October 6. They tell me 'tis my birthday. I am now twenty-two.' He was the fourth son of General Lord Elphinstone, eleventh baron in the peerage of Scotland; and his mother was a daughter of Lord Ruthven.

The Elphinstones take their name from a village near Tranent, in East Lothian, where a tower of the fourteenth or fifteenth century still stands in tolerable preservation. But at this time the family residence was Cumbernauld House, in Dumbartonshire, which had come to Mountstuart's grandfather on his marriage with the heiress of the Flemings, Earls of Wigton, who was also heiress of the Keiths, hereditary earls marischal of Scotland.

Mountstuart was thus descended from ancestors famous in Scottish history. The first baron Elphinstone fell at Flodden; the second at Pinkie. Of the same stock is said to have been that Bishop Elphinstone who founded the University of Aberdeen and introduced the art of printing into Scotland. Another branch of the family was raised to the peerage under the title of Balmerino, which was forfeited for excess of devotion to the House of Stuart. Mountstuart's father had fought under Wolfe in Canada. An uncle, who entered the navy, recovered for the family the title of Baron Keith, in the peerage of Ireland, for his services in the French war. Another uncle, after commanding an East Indiaman, was for thirty-three years a Director of the Company. Of Mountstuart's brothers, the eldest rose to the rank of General, and another (who took the name of Fleming) became Governor of Chelsea Hospital. By such examples was the subject of this memoir encouraged to a life of public service.

His childhood was passed partly at Cumbernauld House, partly at Edinburgh Castle, which his father then occupied as Governor. Home memories of Cumbernauld, with his mother and sisters, are of frequent occurrence in his correspondence; but it is only of his boyish days at Edinburgh that any record has been preserved. Here he used to make friends with the French prisoners in the Castle, learning their revolutionary songs, and wearing his hair long in imitation of their style. All accounts of this early time describe him as characterised by gaiety and love of fun.

In his twelfth year he attended for a short time the High School at Edinburgh, where Francis Horner

EARLY LIFE: ARRIVAL IN INDIA

and the late Lord Murray were among his contemporaries. In 1793, he was sent to a private school of some repute in Kensington. Here he remained for about two years, until his departure for India. As with most boys, his juvenile ambition had been all for the army; but he was quite content with the writership on the Bengal establishment which his uncle the Director procured for him when he was only fifteen years old. His feelings are thus expressed in a letter to his mother, dated March [1795]:

'I am extremely happy to inform you that my uncle has got me appointed to Bengal. On Saturday last he sent for me home, and told me that I was to go with this fleet, which sails in six weeks. He also desired me to apply to writing and ciphering, and to leave off Greek. . . . I am, you may be sure, very happy to be appointed, in spite of all the cockades in the world, which are never to be compared to Bengal. But the worst of all is that I will not be able to return to Scotland for want of time, and so have no possibility of seeing you and my sisters.'

The voyage lasted more than eight months. the ship having been detained at Rio Janeiro (as Clive's ship had been fifty years earlier) and again at Madras. Among his fellow-passengers were two friends of his boyhood:—John Adam, a cousin, son of Chief Commissioner Adam, destined to be for a few months acting Governor-General; and Robert Houston, who became Lieutenant-Governor of the Military College at Addiscombe. They landed at Calcutta on the 26th February, 1796. Sir John Shore (afterwards Lord

Teignmouth) was then Governor-General; and to him, as also to the Commander-in-Chief, Sir Robert Abercromby (a younger brother of Sir Ralph), Mountstuart was warmly commended by his uncle Keith, the admiral. On landing, he was met by an elder brother, James, who had entered the service two years previously, but of whom we hear little more. The two proceeded together to Benares, the journey by water taking two months; though when the Governor-General went up-country a little later—to make preparations against a threatened invasion by the Afgháns under Zemán Sháh—he accomplished the 420 miles in six days.

Benares was then the frontier-station towards the North-West, and an important centre of political affairs. Elphinstone's chief was Mr. Samuel Davis, a civil servant of repute and a Sanskrit scholar; while his brother James was hard by at Ghazípur, under the more famous scholar Colebrooke. It was here that he began his devotion to reading, perhaps under the stimulus of his lifelong friend, Edward Strachey, who was likewise stationed at Benares. Long afterwards, in his diary, under the date of September 24 [1820] he wrote:

'Something put me strongly in mind of the valley near Mirzapur, and of the times when I used to spend days in a cave there, reading Virgil, Horace, and Tibullus.'

Persian he also began at this time, but Greek he did not take up again seriously till much later.

EARLY LIFE: ARRIVAL IN INDIA

Quiet and study at Benares were interrupted by an incident that very nearly cut short Elphinstone's career. Wazír Ali, the deposed Nawáb of Oudh, who was living there under the surveillance of Mr. Cherry, conceived a plot to murder all the English residents at the station. Mr. Cherry and others were cut down on the spot; Mr. Davis retreated to the roof of his house, where he gallantly defended his wife and children, armed only with a spear or pike; Elphinstone and his friend Houston mounted on horseback, and rode for their lives. When order was restored the next day by the troops, Elphinstone received his first diplomatic commission, to trace the complicity of certain suspected natives of high rank. This incident took place in January 1799. The story of it has been told by Sir John Davis, Bart., then a child of a few years old, who afterwards won distinction in China, and survived until 1890 [1].

[1] See *Vizier Ali Khan; or, The Massacre of Benares* (1844), written by Sir J. F. Davis, and dedicated to Mountstuart Elphinstone— a somewhat rare book (with illustrations, and with the historic spear on the cover) a copy of which was presented by Sir J. Davis to the grandfather of the present writer.

CHAPTER III

FIRST APPOINTMENT TO POONA

1801—1802

THE Earl of Mornington (afterwards Marquis Wellesley) had now succeeded Sir John Shore as Governor-General. Among the many grand projects revolving through his mind was the foundation of a college at Calcutta, for the better education of young civilians. This scheme, like others of its author's, failed to gain the approval of the Court of Directors, though it led indirectly to the establishment of Haileybury College, in Hertfordshire. Meanwhile, Lord Wellesley, on his own initiative, opened the short-lived College of Fort William in 1800; and Elphinstone was admitted one of the first students. His stay, however, did not last for many weeks. On the 23rd of January, 1801, he received an offer from Edmonstone, Foreign Secretary to the Governor-General, which gave its colour to the rest of his career. Part of Lord Wellesley's plan at this time was to train young civilians for the diplomatic line by attaching them to the Residents at native courts. Strachey was thus nominated to be secretary to Colonel Kirkpatrick at Poona; and Elphinstone was offered the post of assistant to Strachey, with a salary of Rs. 800 a month. Strange to say, both hesitated about accepting. Elphinstone ultimately decided to abide by the advice of Mr. Davis, which was conveyed in a quotation from Shakspere that 'rang in my ear for the best part of my life':—

> 'What pleasure. sir, find we in life, to lock it
> From action and adventure?'—(*Cymbeline*, Act iv, Sc. 4.)

Then ensued a journey which, in view of modern experience, reads like a romance. Colonel Kirkpatrick fell ill, and we do not hear of him again. But the two young civilians—one aged about 23 and the other only 21—set out for Poona at the head of a numerous cavalcade:

> 'We had eight elephants, eleven camels, four horses, ten bullocks of our own, besides tattoes [ponies] and bullocks belonging to our servants. We had twenty sepoys and from one hundred and fifty to two hundred servants and coolies.'

Such was the apparatus of Indian travel in the first year of the nineteenth century. The route chosen appears yet more extraordinary. Poona lies on the other side of the peninsula, west by south from Calcutta. But our travellers proceeded first along the eastern coast as far as Madras, then inland to Mysore, then north to Haidarábád, and finally west to their destination. By this zigzag course, the distance from Calcutta to Poona, of about 950 miles in a straight line, was extended to nearly twice that distance. Yet more, they loitered on their way at Madras and

Bangalore, and for three months at Haidarábád; so that a journey, which is now accomplished by railway in sixty hours, occupied them altogether nearly a year.

Here are some incidents in this Wanderjahr, during which Elphinstone was unconsciously serving his apprenticeship in Indian diplomacy.

After leaving the British district of Midnapur, the first portion of their journey lay through Orissa, which was then under Marátha rule. They noticed at once a change in the demeanour of the people, who 'were not rude, but showed us no respect.' In the evening they crowded round the encampment, to see the Englishmen go through their exercises, which consisted in throwing the spear, the sword-exercise, and firing at a mark with pistols. At Purí, close to the far-famed Temple of Jagannáth, they met a *fakír* who prophesied the advent of British rule.

'He called us to him and said, "Listen; when will you take this country? This country needs you. The Hindus here are villains, but you are true men. When will you take this country?" We answered, "Never." He said, "Yes: you will certainly take it."'

Within two years the prophecy of the *fakír* was fulfilled.

After passing the Chilka Lake, with the beauty of which they were much taken, they entered the Northern Circars, which had nominally been British territory for about forty years. Nevertheless, our travellers found themselves less secure than in Orissa. Mr.

Brown, the Collector, wrote to them that his province was in complete distraction. Refractory *zamíndárs* were plundering the open country, and burning villages were to be seen on all sides. Mr. Brown sent a Maráthá free-lance, with thirty or forty men, for their protection. Under this foreign escort, they marched through a British province in military array. Even after they had reached the long-settled Karnatik, their troubles were not over. Their palanquins were stopped one night by an English officer, who took them for commercial 'interlopers'; and as they were without passports, they had some difficulty in establishing their identity.

On leaving Madras, Elphinstone laid down in his diary some resolutions to be observed during the remainder of the journey, which—be it remembered—lay almost entirely through Native States.

'I will not scruple to turn out of my way whenever there is a place distinguished for its natural beauty, its buildings, or the remarkable actions of which it has been the scene, even if it should be fifty miles out of the regular road. I will try to observe the produce of the country—the sorts of grain, trees, &c. I will talk as much as I can with the principal people on the modes of collecting revenue and administering justice, and the effects of the acts of our government on the natives.'

In pursuance of these resolutions, Elphinstone spent a month (without Strachey) in visiting the historic sites of Mysore, only two years after the downfall of Tipu. At Seringapatam he was the guest of Colonel

Arthur Wellesley, then in command of the subsidiary force, with whom he was destined to be more intimately associated afterwards.

The two friends arrived together at Haidarábád in the middle of October; and there they spent three months, being introduced to what was then (as it is still) the most magnificent court in India, and being initiated into the secrets of Lord Wellesley's foreign policy. The Resident was Major Kirkpatrick (not to be confounded with the Colonel Kirkpatrick already mentioned), who, three years previously, on the eve of the war with Tipu, had effected the disbandment of the French-trained regiments under Raymond, and had brought the Nizam within the subsidiary system. The success of this undertaking was partly due to Kirkpatrick's personal influence at the native court, but in larger measure to the presence of Malcolm, who had here won his spurs in the field of diplomacy by greatly daring. Kirkpatrick himself was not one from whom Elphinstone could learn much. He belonged to that class of orientalised Europeans, who were not uncommon in the last century; and he had married a daughter of the Persian prime minister. ' His manners were affected, and his conversation most eccentric. He wore moustachios, and dyed his fingers with henna; but in other respects resembled an Englishman.' Elphinstone has left a curious account of his presentation to the Nizam. He was taken by Kirkpatrick through the streets of Haidarábád in great state, with elephants, led horses, infantry, and cavalry. Female sentries were on guard at the doors of the inner palace, and more women were drawn up before a guard-room in sight. 'Kirkpatrick behaved like a native, and with great propriety.'

Elphinstone celebrated his twenty-second birthday at Haidarábád. In his diary he thus records his reflections on the past year, and enumerates the books he had read.

'How pleasantly has the time passed since my last birthday! From the beginning of October to March I lived a studious sort of life, but not the studious sort of life that I lived for the year before at Benares in solitude and depression. . . . Since March I have been on a very agreeable journey; the variety of beautiful scenes and the changes from one agreeable society to another have left no time for tedium. . . .

'I have read since last October a good deal of the history relating to the East—a good deal of Timur's *Institutes*, most part of *The Proceedings of the Secret Committee*, Orme's *Hindustán* (a second time), and Strachey's *Narrative History of Persia*, Sale's *Preliminary Discourse to the Korán*, Jones's *Commentarii*, Revisky on *Hafiz*, some of Gilchrist's *Grammar*. I translated with Strachey a considerable part of an Arabic Grammar, and read Sa'adi's *Gulistán* to p. 38 in Harrington's edition, and a great deal more of his *Bostán*. Of Hafiz, I read 143 Odes in succession, and about as many more here and there; many of them I read many times. I read some of the *Masnavi* of Jaláluddín: not much of books not connected with India. I read a good deal of the *Port Royal Greek Grammar*; an *Odyssey* or two; a few chapters of Herodotus; as much of Hesiod as is in the *Eton Selecta*; the first, seventh, and eighth *Idylls* of Theocritus, and his

Epithalamium of Helen; all of Sappho, Theognis, Callistratus, Bion, Moschus, and Musaeus as are in that collection —(they are most of them scraps); the *Georgics*; all *Phaedrus*; all Horace once over and many parts repeatedly; and a good deal of Petronius. I looked into the Italian Grammar; read the preface and seventy or eighty pages of Tasso; one book of Machiavelli's *History*; a novel and play of his. I also read all Bacon's *Essays*; Hume's *Dialogue on Natural Religion*; Berkeley's essay on *The Principles of Human Knowledge*; Middleton's *Free Enquiry*, his Letter from Rome, several dissertations of his in Latin and English, one volume and a half of his *Cicero*; a good deal of Condorcet on *The Human Understanding*; Tracts by Warburton and 'A Warburtonian'; Warburton on the Sixth Book, from Warton's *Virgil*; some essays of Heyne, at the end of the sixth volume; Denina's *Revolutions of Literature*; Johnson's *Lives* (I had read them before); Boswell's *Life of Johnson*; Voltaire's *Louis XIV*, in English; Aitkin's *Essay on the Use of Natural History*. In poetry, *Paradise Lost* and *Paradise Regained*, all Waller again and again, most of Cowley, Butler, and Denham, Pope and Dryden often; the *Baviad* and the *Maeviad*, Darwin's *Botanic Garden*, *Caractacus*; many of Milton's Latin poems; a great deal of Fontaine; *The Robbers* and two other plays of Schiller; some *Idylls* of Gesner; all Boileau's *Satires*, and a good number of his *Epistles*, and *Mithridate*. I forgot to mention a good deal of Horace Walpole; Jefferson on *Virginia*; Ramsay's *Revolution of South Carolina*; the preface to *Bellendenus*; Japher's *Farriery*; an abstract of St. Pierre's *Études de la Nature*; a Life of Major Geshpill; the *Nation*; and novels innumerable.'

Though based on no system, and revealing but little of the reader's tastes, this long catalogue of titles presents some points of interest. It shows what were the contents of a miscellaneous Indian library at the beginning of the century; and it suggests that a competitive examination may not always be the best means of instilling a love for literature in after life.

It was not until early in 1802 that Elphinstone reached Poona—a place with which his own name will ever be associated in history. Here he found as Resident Colonel (afterwards Sir Barry) Close, a man of very different stamp from Kirkpatrick. An officer in the Madras army, which then supplied more than its proportionate share of 'politicals,' he had won the confidence of Lord Wellesley by the active part he took in the settlement of Mysore. It was from his teaching that Elphinstone first learned to be a supporter of the grand scheme by which the Governor-General was then threatening the independence of the Marátha powers. The circumstance that led to the outbreak of the Second Marátha War must be reserved for a fresh chapter. The present may fitly conclude with some more extracts from Elphinstone's diary, which have no reference to politics.

When presented to the Peshwa, he comments upon the meanness of his court as compared with Haidarábád: 'none of the Marátha chiefs were even like native gentlemen.' Further experience taught him to appreciate Marátha simplicity at a truer valuation.

'How communicative, candid, and sensible Colonel Close is! I do not give attention enough to becoming intimate with him. . . . Talked with Colonel Close about Burke; he

is in love with him. He read some passages from the
Reflections; the assertions seemed to me as false as the
language was beautiful. . . . Some passages of Pope's *Homer*
were mentioned, which I, in silence, compared with the
original. I always feel warmed and inspired by the mention
of Homer; no other author gave me such pleasure in
reading, or left such an impression. . . . A dispute about
the question which is best, the character of the ancients or
moderns. I supported the claims of the former—to magnanimous actions against Desborough, and to eloquence
against the Colonel.'

Meanwhile the clouds of war were gathering close
round Poona, and the crisis of the Marátha confederation was at hand.

CHAPTER IV

THE SECOND MARÁTHÁ WAR

1802—1803

AT this time—when Tipu had fallen, and the Nizam of Haidarábád and also the Nawáb of Oudh had meekly accepted the treaties forced on them—the Maráthás were the only native power remaining independent in India. Lord Wellesley, in pursuance of his resolute policy to make the British paramount throughout the peninsula, was determined to impose the subsidiary system upon the Maráthás also. This idea was not welcome to all his lieutenants, not even to his brother Arthur. But the Governor-General himself never wavered, being greatly influenced by fear lest the French officers in Maráthá service should furnish local support for an invasion by Napoleon. At first, he tried diplomatic pressure; but his proposals were rejected by both Sindia and the Bhonsla Rájá of Nágpur, nor did they meet with much more acceptance at Poona. Just when it seemed that Lord Wellesley would be compelled to commence hostilities, a fortunate turn of events enabled him to shift the responsibility for aggression upon the Maráthás. The treaty of Bassein, which placed the Peshwa in his power, was the direct cause of the Second Marátha War.

The reigning Peshwa—the last of his line—was Bájí Ráo, still young in years, but surrounded from childhood by an atmosphere of treachery, bloodshed, and anarchy. The military supremacy had passed to the rival houses of Sindia and Holkar, who fought a series of battles for the possession of the capital and the person of the Peshwa, whom they still affected to regard as their national chief. When Elphinstone arrived at Poona, in the beginning of 1802, the influence of Sindia was in the ascendant. Just a little earlier, the Peshwa had condemned Vitují Holkar, who had fallen into his hands, to a horrible death: he was tied to the foot of an elephant and thus dragged through the streets of the city. To avenge this outrage on his brother, Jeswant Ráo Holkar collected a large army, with which he defeated Sindia's French-trained battalions, and appeared before Poona. The Peshwa sought the protection of the British, but in vain; for he was not yet humbled enough to accept the subsidiary system, which alone Close was empowered to offer. In the decisive battle fought outside Poona on the 25th of October, 1802, Holkar was again victorious. The Peshwa fled to the Konkan, whither he was followed by Colonel Close. He was now willing to consent to any conditions, provided he could recover his throne. On the last day of the year he signed the treaty of Bassein, which aimed a fatal blow at Marátha independence. By one of its terms the Peshwa agreed to have no diplomatic relations except through the Pritish Resident. That the other Maráthá Chiefs should acquiesce in the degradation of the head of their race, was impossible; nor is it likely that Bájí Ráo himself intended to be bound longer than he could help. But the Governor-General had made all his preparations for such an emergency, and welcomed the war that followed. General Arthur Wellesley, his brother, was ordered to advance northwards from Mysore, and restore the Peshwa. This he did by forced marches, accomplishing the last sixty miles into Poona within thirty-two hours. Holkar retired before him, and for the time remained quiet in his dominions. But Sindia and the Bhonsla Rájá of Nágpur refused to accept the new order of things, and moved their allied forces into the Deccan, menacing both Poona and Haidarábád.

After some months of idle negotiation, which allowed the English to perfect their military plans, war was declared early in August, 1803. Lord Lake, the Commander-in-Chief, with about 16,000 men, was entrusted with the task of expelling Sindia's disciplined battalions under French command from Hindustán proper. Another army of equal strength, divided between General Arthur Wellesley and General Stevenson, operated against the combined forces of Sindia and the Bhonsla in the Deccan; while a smaller army was detached for the invasion of Orissa, then part of the Nágpur State. Brilliant success attended each of the three campaigns. Before the end of the year both Sindia and the Bhonsla were compelled to accept hard conditions of peace, which stripped them of large tracts of territory, and left them comparatively harmless for the future. Holkar forthwith took up arms; and, with divided counsels, victory was no longer chained to the English standards. The disastrous retreat of Colonel Monson through Central India pursued by Holkar, and Lord Lake's repulse before the earthen walls of Bhartpur, tarnished our military fame; while the abandonment of the Rájput princes and other allies to the tender mercies of Holkar and his Pindárís, impaired our reputation for good faith. Lord Wellesley, however, had left India before this final humiliation.

So much of introduction is necessary in order to explain the part which Elphinstone played in this great drama. His diary is interrupted at this time, so that we have no description of the crisis at Poona from his pen. But it is certain that he was throughout by the side of Colonel Close, when he hastened after the Peshwa through the passes of the Western Gháts. Later letters show that he had contracted an obstinate liver-complaint when at Bombay and Bassein during the cold season of 1802–3. However, he accompanied Colonel Close back to Poona, when the Peshwa was formally re-instated by troops from Bombay on the 13th of May, 1803. General Wellesley had now taken the field, to watch the threatening armaments of Sindia and the Bhonsla. The political agent with his army was Malcolm, his intimate friend, and the most trusted lieutenant of the Governor-General.

But in August, just before active hostilities began, Malcolm fell ill, to his own exceeding chagrin, and Elphinstone was deputed to take his place. It was impossible that he could at once step into Malcolm's position as the confidential adviser of the general in diplomatic matters; and his duties seem to have been ill-defined. After the war was over, it was decided that he should draw the allowances of a secretary. But General Wellesley always wrote his own dispatches, and conducted his negotiations in person. Elphinstone's linguistic attainments were utilised as an interpreter in Persian, Maráthi, and 'Moors'—the usual name at this time for Hindustáni—and as the head of a not very efficient intelligence department. He does not appear to have been hardly worked; and he probably enjoyed this brief and brilliant campaign more than any other period of his life. In his old age he often talked with pride of having been initiated into warfare by the Great Duke.

He joined the camp on the 10th of August, 1803, just a week after war had been declared. General Wellesley was then besieging the fortress of Ahmadnagar, reputed to be impregnable; but after two days' bombardment, the garrison capitulated. Elphinstone's literary predilections are curiously revealed in the letter he wrote to his friend Strachey, who remained with Close at Poona:

'Nothing has been sold but swords. I enquired about books, and heard of an Arabic prayer-book, which I might have got for you if it had not been restored to the owner, a very famous Dervish, who predicted on the day of the attack that our army would take the fort in nine *gharis* [hours].'

By the capture of Ahmadnagar, the Peshwa's dominions were secured from invasion. General Wellesley's next care was to protect the territory of the Nizam, and, if possible, to force the enemy to fight. About a month was consumed in a series of zigzag marches, the position of the enemy from day to day being concealed by a cloud of Pindárí horse, until at last they were discovered on the further side of a little river, near the village of Assaye (now in the Nizam's Dominions). The Maráthá army consisted of some 30,000 irregular cavalry, 10,000 disciplined troops, and about 100 guns well served. General Wellesley had only about 4500 men, of whom one regiment of cavalry and two of infantry were Europeans. But he did not hesitate to attack immediately, without waiting for the co-operation of Stevenson, who was distant about eight miles. The battle was most hotly contested, being a succession of cavalry and infantry charges in the face of a heavy fire. More than once the issue seemed doubtful, and it has been said that under any other commander Assaye would have been a British defeat. But Wellesley conducted in person the several movements of horse, foot, and artillery, and everywhere inspired victory by his presence. At last the Maráthás fled in disorder, leaving all their guns behind them. But the victory was dearly purchased. One English regiment lost 400 out of its complement of 500 men; and the total of killed and wounded amounted to more than one-third of the entire force.

Elphinstone rode by the side of Wellesley throughout the day, being one of two on the staff who were untouched either in their persons or their horses. His intelligent appreciation of the tactics is shown in a detailed description of the battle (with a plan), which has been of use to military historians. One incident is worth quotation for its vivid telling :

'The line advanced under a very hot cannonade. When we got near enough the enemy to hear them shout, the General rode back to the cavalry, whom he had sent for, and who were now in the rear. He rode full gallop, told Colonel Maxwell to take care of the right of the infantry, and rode back at speed. In coming back as in going, there was the *Divil's own* cannonade (an exquisite Irish phrase which I have found out), and three horses of our party were knocked down. The General galloped forward to a line which was before us, and we were getting near it very fast when it fired a gun our way: we were barely out of musket-shot. Somebody said, "Sir! that is the enemy's line." The General said, "Is it? Ha! damme, so it is!" (you know his manner) and turned.'

The following is a more characteristic example of Elphinstone's style. It was written ten days after the battle, for so long was the victorious army halted on the spot :

'There was a Roman Emperor [Vitellius] who said he liked the smell of a dead enemy. If he did, he was singular in his taste. We are horribly perfumed with such a smell as he liked, but I would rather smell a living enemy. I went yesterday evening to the field of battle. It was a dark, cloudy evening. I rode by myself, and saw *plurima mortis imago*. Some of the dead are withered, their features still remaining, but their faces blackened to the colour of coal; others still swollen and blistered. . . . I saw a black dog tearing in a furious way great pieces of flesh from a dead man, looking fiercely and not regarding me. I thought the group horrible and sublime. At last I began to feel a good deal of horror —awful, but not unpleasant—when by way of adding to the sublimity the evening gun fired, and to my surprise I heard a ball whistle over my head.'

The pursuit after Assaye was entrusted to Stevenson's force, while Wellesley continued his strategy of marching and countermarching, to prevent the enemy from over-running the friendly territories of the Peshwa or the Nizam. Here is the account of a 'camp day' as described by Elphinstone at this time:—

'General at half-past four. Tent-pins rattle, and I rise and dress while they are striking my tent. Go to the front, and to the Quartermaster-General's tent, and drink a cup of tea. Talk with the *état-major*, who collect there till it grows light. The assembly beats and the General comes out. We go to his breakfast-table in front of his tent and breakfast; talk all the time. It is bitter cold [November 15], and we have our great-coats on. At half after six, or earlier or later, we mount and ride. . . . The General generally rides on the dusty flank, so nobody stays with him. Now we always . . . have coursing a mile or so out on the flank; and when we get to our ground from ten to twelve we all sit, if our chairs have come up, or lie on the ground. . . . When the tent is pitched, we move in, and the General lies on the carpet, and we all talk, &c., till breakfast is ready. Then we breakfast off fried mutton, mutton-chops, curries, &c., and from eleven to two get to our tents, and I arrange my *harkáras* [messengers], write my journals, read Puffendorf, Lysias [?], and write you [Strachey] and Adam, and sometimes talk politics and other privitie with the General. And then at two or three I eat a loaf and drink two glasses of port-and-water. And when it grows dark ... I get shaved, and walk about headquarters line till it is pitch dark, and then dress, go to dinner; and we all talk about the march, &c., and they about their former wars and this war, and Indian courts, and politics, &c. At nine we break up; and the Quartermaster-General and Major of Brigade and I hold a committee, and settle whether [? whither] we march next day; and then I go to palanquin. All this is extremely pleasant. I have enjoyed—I mean relished—society, and study, and business, and action, and adventure, all according to their several natures.'

Meanwhile it seemed as if Lake's series of crushing victories in Hindustán would have ended the war. Sindia was already disposed to sue for peace; but the resistance of the Bhonsla was not yet broken, and more fighting remained for Elphinstone to witness. On the 29th of November, just two months after Assaye, the enemy was again encountered on the wide plain that takes its name from the little village of Argáum, in Berár. The greater part were under the command of the brother of the Bhonsla, including a picked regiment of Arab infantry—who seem, indeed, throughout the Marátha wars to have proved more formidable than the French-trained battalions; while Sindia contributed a large body of horse. On the side of the English, Wellesley and Stevenson had now joined their forces. The battle did not begin until late in the afternoon. At first, the Sepoys, who had been so staunch at Assaye, were thrown into confusion by the heavy cannonade, until rallied by Wellesley in person. A European regiment encountered the Arabs; while Wellesley led his Madras cavalry against the Marátha horse, who offered but a feeble resistance. Before sunset the enemy were in full flight, while the loss on the English side was insignificant. 'If we had had daylight an hour more, not a man would have escaped.'

Elphinstone again rode by the side of his General, and took part in the cavalry charge.

'The balls knocked up the dust under our horses' feet. I had no narrow escapes this time; and I felt quite unconcerned, never winced, nor cared how near the shot came about the worst time. And all the while I was at pains to see how the people looked, and every gentleman seemed at ease as much as if he were riding a-hunting. . . . The dragoons used their swords for some time and then drew their pistols. . . . I saw nobody afterwards but people on foot, whom I did not think it proper to touch. Indeed, there is nothing very gallant in attacking routed and terrified horse, who have not presence of mind either to run or fight.'

On his visit to the battle-field next morning, Elphinstone picked up a wounded Hindustáni, who had, it turned out, been servant to Cherry at Benares, and who henceforth continued in Elphinstone's service until he left India.

THE SECOND MARÁTHÁ WAR 41

The war was now over, so far as opposition in the field was concerned. Both Sindia and the Bhonsla were willing to accept the British terms. But the obstinacy of the *killadár*, or commandant, of the hill-fortress of Gáwalgarh served to supply Elphinstone with one more phase of fighting. One would have thought that his time would have been fully occupied with the negotiations for peace, which were now being conducted daily with an envoy from the Bhonsla. Nothing, however, would satisfy him but to be present at the storm, which was under the direction, not of his own General, but of Stevenson. He met with his usual luck in escaping unhurt, though he ran an additional risk by not wearing uniform, so that he might have been taken for 'a European of the enemy's.' The following has a unique interest, as being a description of a storm by one who took part in it, who was both a philosopher and an historian:

'Breakfasted with Kennedy, and talked about Hafiz, Sa'adi, Horace, and Anacreon. At nine I left him and went to the trenches. . . . I went up to Colonel Kenny, said I heard he was to lead the storming party, and that if he would allow me, I would be of his party. He bowed and agreed. . . . We drew our swords, stuck pistols in our belts or handkerchiefs tied round our middle, and passing in rear of the batteries marched on to the breach. . . . Then followed the Ninety-fourth Regiment. Our advance was silent, deliberate, and even solemn. Everybody expected the place to be well defended. . . . Our cannon fired over our heads. We got to the breach, where we halted and let the forlorn hope, a sergeant's party, run up. Then we followed, ran

along, and dashed up the second breach and huzzaed. . . .
Soon after the troops poured in, so that there was no
distinguishing forlorn hope or anything. . . . Such of the
enemy as stood were put to the bayonet; but most of them
ran off to the right, and down a narrow valley which led to a
gate. Here they met Colonel Chalmers coming on with half
the Seventy-eighth; the Ninety-fourth pressed behind, firing
from above, and a terrible slaughter took place. After this
we endeavoured to push on, when, to our astonishment, we
discovered that we had only gained a separate hill, and that
the fort lay behind a deep valley, beyond which appeared a
double wall and strong gates. The troops halted, and the
officers endeavoured to form them. . . . But Colonel Kenny,
almost alone, had run on to the gate, where he was now
perceived. The Europeans found the road down and crowded
after him. . . . Beyond the first wall was a narrow rocky
road, overtopped by a steep rock, and another wall and gate.
. . . While the Europeans were clambering over, the enemy
kept up a fire from their works. In the meantime our
people poured in at the breach, and covered the hill opposite
to the enemy. They fired on the enemy, and the valley was
filled with such a roar of musketry as can hardly be conceived. At last our men got over, and opened the first gate.
Scaling ladders were got up the hill, and applied to the
second wall. The enemy fled from their works; we rushed
over the wall, and the fort was ours. . . . Johnson and I
endeavoured to collect a party to push for the gate where
General Wellesley's division was. This was easy; the officers
were all obliging, and every man you spoke to joined you,
and a prisoner was taken who knew the way. But here
began the difficulty. Every step there was something to
lead away your people; the enemy, plunder, water, or some
strange sight stopped us on every side. We picked up new
parties, and pushed on till the *killadár's* house stopped

even ourselves. All around us lay dead and dying, and on one side was an officer calling out for volunteers to hang the *killadár*. I saved him by the argument that he knew where the treasure was. . . .

'When we went on to the breach, I thought I was going to a great danger; but my mind was so made up to it that I did not care for anything. The party going to the storm put me in mind of the eighth and ninth verses of the third book of Homer['s Iliad]:

οἳ δ' ἄρ' ἴσαν σιγῇ μένεα πνείοντες Ἀχαιοὶ,
ἐν θυμῷ μεμαῶτες ἀλεξέμεν ἀλλήλοισιν.

And after one gets over the breach, one is too busy and animated to think of anything but how to get on. So much for Gáwalgarh.'

Gáwalgarh was taken on the 15th of December. On the following day Malcolm arrived in camp, in time to take part in the final arrangements for peace. The actual treaty was dictated by Elphinstone to the Persian writers that very night, and was signed on the evening of the next day by the agent of the Bhonsla. The peace with Sindia, known in history as the Treaty of Surji Anjangáon, was not finally settled until thirteen days later, the 30th of December, 1803.

Thus ended the most stirring chapter in Elphinstone's life. Within the space of little more than four months he had been present at two pitched battles and two regular sieges, as the confidential secretary of one who not only became the foremost captain of his time, but who had also thus early manifested his talents for statesmanship. As before mentioned,

Arthur Wellesley gave Elphinstone the testimonial, that he had mistaken his profession and ought to have been a soldier. What was of more importance to Elphinstone at the time, he obtained for him the appointment of Resident at the court of the Bhonsla; and he thus wrote of him in an official letter to his brother, the Governor-General:

'Upon the occasion of mentioning Mr. Elphinstone, it is but justice to that gentleman to inform your Excellency that I have received the greatest assistance from him since he has been with me. He is well versed in the language, has experience and knowledge of the Marátha powers, and their relations with each other and with the British Government and its allies. He has been present in all the actions which have been fought in this quarter during the war, and at all the sieges. He is acquainted with every transaction that has taken place, and with my sentiments upon all subjects. I therefore take the liberty of recommending him to your Excellency.'

CHAPTER V

NÁGPUR, AND SINDIA'S CAMP

1804—1808

THE recommendation of General Wellesley won for Elphinstone, at the early age of twenty-four, one of the prizes of Indian service—the Residency of Nágpur, with a salary of Rs. 3000 a month. Nominally, he was sent as secretary to Mr. Josiah Webbe, a veteran diplomatist on the civil establishment at Madras. But Webbe, as was anticipated, never took up his appointment, and died within a year at the court of Sindia. It is again curious to learn that the young man was not elated by his rapid advancement. His rough life in the camp had not unnaturally inspired him with a desire to revisit his friends at Calcutta and to enjoy the company of ladies. In an epigram worthy of Sir Henry Wotton, he wrote: 'Conceive what society there will be where people speak what they don't think in Moors.' But, in truth, he was now entering upon the second stage of his apprenticeship, which qualified him for the performance of his master-work at Poona.

Elphinstone was certainly under no illusion with

regard to the arduous nature of his new duties. Unlike Malcolm, who was ever sanguine of the future and prone to trust in native promises, his temperament tended to be pessimistic, as regards both his own abilities and the course of politics. None knew better the hollowness of the peace that had concluded the Second Marátha War. While always prepared for a fresh outbreak, he considered it wisest to postpone the evil day as long as possible. Concerning the result, if matters should be brought to the arbitrament of arms, he never entertained the slightest apprehension; but what he seems to have dreaded, even in these early days, was a too rapid extension of British conquest.

His chief difficulty at the moment was about 'intelligence,' in other words, espionage, the importance of which had been impressed upon him by General Wellesley.

'I do not get on well about intelligence. It appears to me indispensable to try every way to get it, because this man's [the Rájá's] character makes it probable he will conspire to involve us in another war. If we know of his machinations, I believe it possible to defeat them without force. If we do not, we must have a contest which will end in his ruin. Yet I do not like the ways in which intelligence is obtained. I hate anything that is secret and indirect, and abhor to do what I should be unwilling to avow. If the Rájá discovered that I was enquiring into the situation of his armies and the intrigues of his court, what should I say? I should avow it, and tell him that he had once brought down a dangerous war on us in the middle of a profound peace, that afterwards we should want prudence and attention to the welfare of our country if we neglected to watch him.'

And again, in words that seem to re-echo another lesson learnt from General Wellesley:

'I must never forget to be always and absolutely open. If I try cunning management, I act contrary to my own character and that of my nation, and perhaps fail after all. My diplomatic motto ought to be—

'Εχθρὸς γάρ μοι κεῖνος ὁμῶς 'Αΐδαο πύλῃσιν,
"Ος χ' ἕτερον μὲν κεύθῃ ἐνὶ φρεσὶν, ἄλλο δὲ βάζει.'

Elphinstone remained altogether four years at Nágpur—from January, 1804, to April, 1808—broken by a trip to Calcutta. This was an anxious period in Indian affairs, though none of the troubles directly affected Nágpur. It falls within four Governor-Generalships—the last year of Lord Wellesley; the two brief months of Lord Cornwallis's second term; the inglorious rule of Sir George Barlow; and the arrival of Lord Minto. In Indian history this period is remembered for the reversal of Lord Wellesley's policy of making the British supreme throughout the peninsula by means of exclusive alliances with the native powers. The tide had turned even before Lord Wellesley left the country. Indeed, the conclusion of the Second Marátha War, despite its brilliant successes in the field, marked the beginning of the ebb. Neither Sindia nor the Bhonsla, though acknowledging themselves beaten, would accept a subsidiary force, which, with the example of the Nizam and the Peshwa before their eyes, they re-

garded as a sign of the loss of independence. The
third great Marátha Chief, Holkar, now tried the
chances of the sword; and though defeated in the
end, he managed to inflict upon the English two
disasters from which their military reputation in
India long suffered — the ignominious retreat of
Monson and Lake's failure to take Bhartpur. More
pregnant of future mischief than these accidents of
war was the peace offered to Holkar. Not only was
he permitted to retain all his territory, but the ancient
princes of Rájputána, who had lent assistance to the
English, were abandoned to his mercy. Sindia naturally fretted at the favourable terms which his rival
had received, until he too was appeased by the restoration of some of his lost possessions. Finally, British
prestige suffered yet another blow in the mutiny of
Madras sepoys at Vellore, which was accompanied
by plots for a similar outbreak at Haidarábád.

These events could not but tend to weaken Elphinstone's influence at Nágpur, and to depress his own
spirits. In his letters at this period we hear occasionally of political troubles, such as the disinclination of the Rájá to give up portions of the territory
surrendered by treaty, or his repeated objections to a
subsidiary force. On more than one occasion Elphinstone had to threaten a renewal of hostilities before
he could frustrate the designs of the war party at
Nágpur. But his diplomacy at the most critical
period was so successful as to win high encomiums
from Lord Wellesley.

Here is an episode that strikingly illustrates the kind of men with whom he had to deal.

'I recommended to Jeswant Rámchandra [the minister] that some freebooters who had laid waste, plundered, slaughtered, and destroyed should be punished. His answer is a mirror of slavish ideas and Hindustáni manners. It was that "he knew the English put people to death for such offences, but his Highness shudders at the name of an execution." Once when he had returned from a certain place a servant whose duty it was to wash the Rájá's hands did it with scalding water. Everyone was for putting him and the *jamadár* he was under to death, but the Rájá forgave them both. Another time when he came to want water, he found that, through the neglect of his servant, his *lota* [pot] was filled with *ghi*. The servant was sent for: all called out to have him executed immediately, and Pandurang, Bakhshí's brother, was going to kill him on the spot; but the Rájá said, "Let him go: it is easy to kill a man, but not so to make another."'

We now begin to hear a good deal about the Pindárís, whose ravages were allowed, through the supineness of the British Government, to be the scourge of the Deccan for ten years longer. These freebooters, who had their home in Central India under the protection of Sindia and Holkar, inherited the customs and traditions of the early Maráthás under Sivají. Mounted on hardy ponies, they used to sweep through the Deccan from sea to sea in large bands, harrying the defenceless husbandmen at the spear's point, and carrying back stores of booty to their distant camps. To this day many villages in the Maráthá country

D

recall the memory of the Pindárís by their walls or hedges of prickly pear. Their audacity was so great that they paid no regard to the armies of the native powers, and were scarcely to be deterred by the presence of a British detachment. Their rapidity of movement was extraordinary.

'Wallace states them to have marched six days and nights without any regular halt to surprise Amráoti [then a great native capital, now famous as a mart for raw cotton]. Yet such was their speed and bottom, that the very day they were beat off from Amráoti, a party of those who attacked it arrived at Bozar, sixty miles from that town; and in eight days from the time they left the hills till their return they plundered the whole left bank of the Wárdha, down as far as Chanda, sending parties as far east as Kuí, which is fifteen miles E. S. E. of this place [Nágpur].'

Twice they came close to Nágpur, where the Rájá had no force available to resist them. 'Neither Jack Straw at London Stone, nor Holkar at Poona, ever caused such an alarm.' It is characteristic of Elphinstone that his only fear was lest he should lose his valued books, which were destined afterwards to be burnt at Poona. On another occasion, when he was on the march with only twenty-five *sawárs* (native troopers), Elphinstone himself had a narrow escape. A party of about 5000 Pindárís swept a great part of the road he had just traversed, and carried off a tent and some camels that were coming on in the rear. The servants captured at the time were all released in the end.

'They described the behaviour of the Pindárís as by no means so fierce and brutal as it is said to be. They neither wounded nor hurt anybody. They enquired where I was; some threatened me, while others said they were willing to serve us if we could be prevailed on to entertain them.'

But, on the whole, Elphinstone's life at Nágpur was one of tranquillity, and even of loneliness, which he alleviated by out-of-door amusements as well as by study. We now first hear of his taking up the native sports of hawking and coursing: hog-hunting seems to have followed later, at Poona. In one letter he claims to have 'flushed and dropped the first five brace of snipe ever killed' near Nágpur, on the morning of the Pindárí scare. In another letter he gives a long account of an unsuccessful tiger-hunt, in company with Jenkins, which is memorable in the annals of Indian *shikár* for the fact that, when their elephants became unmanageable through fear, they 'called for camels.' He built for himself a bungalow some few miles in the country, which he called Falconer's Hall; but this was intended more for quiet reading than for sport.

The Persian poets first engaged his attention, forming a congenial subject of correspondence with his old friend Jenkins, now Resident with Sindia. After a while, however, he laid them aside, on account of his belief of their pernicious effects on the mind. 'You know I always maintained that they were the source of blue devils.' One criticism of his is of interest at the present day. 'Khayyám is a singular writer. His epigrams are far above any of those that I have read in Greek or Latin (which, by the way, are about a dozen). They are bold and very often profound thoughts in forcible language.' He now took up Greek in earnest, which he had almost dropped since the Benares days. After going through the Iliad, he read most of the plays of Sophocles, occasionally diverging to Theocritus and Tyrtaeus. This was preliminary to a course of Greek history, beginning with Thucydides (for whom he expresses the highest admiration), and continued through Xenophon and several Speeches of Demosthenes. He was fortunate in finding companions among his visitors, notably Jenkins and Close, to encourage him in these severe studies, which were relieved, about this time, by the arrival of a box of books from England, which included *The Lay of the Last Minstrel*. He devoured it with delight, and frequently quotes from it in his subsequent letters.

In January, 1807, he started for Calcutta, on a year's leave of absence. He took the direct route across the forest-clad and almost unexplored hill-country of Chutia Nágpur; and was careful to provide himself, not only with an escort, but also with a plentiful supply of books. It was probably on this occasion that he formed a collection of the dialects spoken by the hill-tribes, at the suggestion of Sir James Mackintosh; but this anticipation of the labours of the missionary Hislop has unhappily not been preserved. His new interest in field-sports led him to make enquiries also about the wild beasts, which still abound in these jungles.

'From the *patél* [head-man] I learned that the villagers in this forest [near Patargáon] are greatly distressed by the wild buffaloes that destroy their fields. They come in herds of five hundred head, and if ten or a dozen are shot the rest are not intimidated. They are very hard to kill: no arrow has any effect on them: even four or five shots from a matchlock, which would easily kill a tiger, often fail with them. . . . They are far larger than common buffaloes. There is an account of a similar kind called the *gaur* [bison]; one distinction between it and the buffalo is the length of its hoofs.'

Again, in the Gond chiefship of Chhota Udaipur:

'I talked with the Gond about killing tigers. They do it with arrows poisoned with a low plant called *mahuna*, which is fastened in the arrow. A tiger dies of the wound in a few hours. They would use the same poison in all their wars, were it not for the expense. As it is, each man has one and some two. A good archer here cannot hit further than at fifty paces.'

At Calcutta, Elphinstone had the advantage of making the personal acquaintance of the new Governor-General, Lord Minto, who received him cordially, though some traces are apparent of a traditionary feud between the two Lowland families. Elphinstone's name for him in letters is 'Gibby Elliot,' or 'the Laird of Stobbs'; while his former honoured chief, Lord Wellesley, is opprobriously styled 'Old Villainy.' Of his stay at Calcutta nothing is recorded, beyond his enjoyment of the society of English ladies, whom he had scarcely seen for six years. 'Such lots of women, and laughing, and philandering that I was in heaven.'

His return journey, 'after the roads were open in December,' was accomplished in a roundabout way by sea to Masulipatam, and thence *via* Haidarábád and Ellichpur. At the latter place, he was magnificently entertained by Nawáb Salábat Khán, the deputy of the Nizam; and it is easy to see that Elphinstone always felt more at ease in the company of Muhammadans than of Hindus. In April, 1808, about a month after his return to Nágpur, he received orders to relieve Mercer, the successor of Jenkins at the court of Sindia, who had fallen ill; and at the same time we first hear of a vague desire to be entrusted with a mission to Afghánistán.

In the middle of the hot weather, he set off *via* Jabalpur and Ságar, to reach Sindia's camp.

He thus describes his march:—

'At eight or nine I rise and breakfast, then write my journal, inquire about the country, &c., and receive visits from Sindia's and the Bhonsla's *sardárs* [nobles]. I then read Polybius and Gurbert's *Tactics* till near three, dress— viz. put on a shirt, pair of boots, coat, pantaloons, and neckcloth—in about two-and-a-half minutes; dine at three. At four retire to a tree, have four *tattis* [moistened mats] put up round my chair. At five set off, go on an elephant (to see the country) till dark; then mount and ride till eleven, one, or five o'clock, according as the march consists of twelve, sixteen, or twenty-two miles, generally till one; then sup while the tents are pitching, and go to bed. . . . I have a camel-load and a half of books, packed with such exquisite art as to be both perfectly secure and perfectly come-at-able.'

After crossing the Narbadá, Elphinstone was much struck by the change.

'The country, the people, the language, everything quite different from those of the Deccan side. . . . This is quite Hindustán. *Zamindárs* [land-owners] come to visit us, and threaten to fire on our Marátha horse if they enter their villages.'

He was still more impressed by the signs everywhere visible of the ravages of Sindia's troops. Though the country was fertile, villages were lying waste, and even towns were half in ruins. This was not the result of anarchy or of war, but only of Sindia's method of revenue-collection. Like a true Marátha, he was moving about his dominions with a large army of irregulars, levying tribute in kind at the spear's point.

At last Elphinstone reached Sindia's camp—he seems to have resided at no permanent capital, for Gwalior had been but lately ceded to him—somewhere on the borders of Rájputána; and he wrote of it the following vivid description to his sister :—

'Conceive a king and his court, with all their servants and retinue, a very small army of regular infantry and irregular cavalry, and a collection of shopkeepers and every other description of people that is found in a town, the whole amounting to 150,000 men, crowded into a camp in which all pitch in confusion, in all kinds and sizes of tents; add one great street with shops of all kinds in tents on each side of

it, and, in the middle of the whole, one great enclosure
of canvas walls containing a great number of tents for the
accommodation of Sindia and his family; and this will give
you as clear a notion of a Marátha camp as it is possible to
have of so confused a thing. Now figure the same people
with their tents and baggage loaded on elephants, camels,
bullocks, and ponies, all mixed up together and straggling
over the country, for fifteen miles in length and two or three
in breadth; and you have a notion of the same army
marching. The confusion of the government is greater than
that of the camp or line of march. When I arrived, Sindia
and all his Ministers were confined [*dharna*] by a body of
troops, who had mutinied for pay. The Ministers were kept
without eating; but the prince, who was allowed to do as he
pleased, was very little affected by the state of affairs, and
spent his days very comfortably in playing cards with his
favourites. . . . In this way Sindia wanders over all the
centre of Hindustán, levying his own revenue, and plundering
his weaker neighbours, with no variety except that he sometimes halts during the rainy season, sometimes has a fort to
besiege, and sometimes a battle to fight.'

Of the prince himself, Elphinstone formed a not
unfavourable opinion, though strongly prejudiced
against him because of his ill-treatment of Jenkins.
He thought him weak rather than vicious: 'his
conduct depends on the character of his Minister, and
not on his own.' After his first state interview, he
thus describes his personal appearance:

'Sindia is a man of thirty-one [three years older than
Elphinstone himself]; he looks about twenty-three. He is
not tall, but stout and well-proportioned. He has rather a
lively and agreeable face, though his features are low, and

his countenance something of the Malay. If he were not a prince, he would strike one as a smart young Maratha. He had on a very rich necklace (pearls and emeralds): there were a great many strings twisted up together, and put on like a neckcloth. He had also valuable pearls in his ears.'

On one occasion Sindia took him for a tiger-hunt, into which Malcolm would have entered with more zest than Elphinstone, who was content to be a spectator of the prince's skill with the gun. He expresses himself, however, as much delighted with the sport: and he observes that the manners of the hunting party were free and agreeable. 'People talked directly to Sindia, and conversation went on well.' Of serious politics we hear nothing. The position of a Resident was then very different from what it is now. Not only was he unconcerned with the internal administration, however anarchical; he was not even called upon to say a word about foreign affairs, unless British interests came directly in question. Sindia had just sent an army into the Rájput State of Jaipur, which the reversal of Wellesley's policy had abandoned to the Maráthás. But Holkar claimed Jaipur as his own special preserve: and it seemed probable that war would result between the two ancient rivals. Yet Elphinstone did not feel it his duty to remonstrate, much less to interfere.

In truth, during the two months that Elphinstone was in Sindia's camp, his thoughts were elsewhere. For the first time in his life, his latent ambition had been awakened by the hope that he might win renown in the wider arena of international diplomacy by a successful mission to Afghánistán. His dream was, as that of Wellesley had been, to bring the influence of India to bear upon the great drama which was at this time centring round the relations of France and Russia, and to associate his own name, however remotely, with the overthrow of Napoleon.

At last, on July 10 (1808), he received the welcome news of his appointment, with instructions to proceed at once to Delhi. The very next evening he set off, travelling at the rate of forty miles a day, and leaving even his books behind him. His route lay through Bundelkhand, a wild country of which the inhabitants were accustomed both to plundering and to being plundered. 'Though all the villagers were ready on their towers, and ordered us to pass them by a certain road, none refused us guides.' His haste did not prevent him from devoting one day to the wonders of Agra. He viewed with respect the shrine that holds the dust of Akbar; but he was disappointed with the Táj. At Delhi, he seems to have met for the first time Metcalfe—who was making preparations for a similar mission to the court of Ranjít Singh at Lahore —'a mild, good-natured, clever, enterprising fellow, able and willing for anything.' The Resident at Delhi was Seton, whose chief duty was to take charge of the blind old Emperor, Sháh Alam, but recently released from his Marátha jailors. With Seton Elphinstone was instructed to concert all the arrangements for his embassy to Kábul.

CHAPTER VI

THE KÁBUL MISSION

1808 —1810.

THE high hopes with which Elphinstone started on his mission to Kábul were doomed to disappointment. He never reached Afghánistán proper; the Sháh with whom he negotiated was driven from his throne before ever the treaty was ratified; and no permanent results ensued, either for good or evil, to British interests. It was not until after a lapse of thirty years that any fresh attempt was made to re-open relations with the Afgháns. In the career of Elphinstone, too, the Kábul mission was a mere episode, upon which in after years he looked back with mingled feelings. He used to say that it entirely cured him of ambition. But it also contributed not a little to widen his experience and strengthen his sense of responsibility; it brought his name before the public at home, and it ultimately launched him into literature.

The mission to Kábul formed but one part of a comprehensive scheme of diplomacy, conceived by Lord Minto on a scale not unworthy of the Marquis Wellesley. The chief object of Wellesley, in making the English supreme throughout the peninsula, had been to prevent the French from obtaining a foothold at any of the native courts. So now, again, the foreign policy of Minto was inspired by dread of a French invasion. But this time it was from beyond the frontier, not from within, that danger was anticipated.

In 1808, Napoleon had reached the zenith of his power, and stood forth as the undisputed master of continental Europe. Spain, Italy, and Holland had long been vassal states; Austria and Prussia both lay crushed; Russia was recently bound by the fetters of the Peace of Tilsit. All the known circumstances seemed to justify the belief that Napoleon would now seek a new world to conquer in the Far East, where alone he could feed fat his ancient grudge against the English name. The Sultan of Turkey was already his subservient ally; and, despite the exertions of Malcolm, French influence had become predominant at the court of the Shâh of Persia. General Gardane was now sent to Teherán, with a brilliant staff and a strong escort, ostensibly to prepare the way for a joint invasion of India by Persian and French armies. It has even been affirmed that the Gomal Pass was selected as the route by which the invaders should descend from Afghánistán upon the plain of the Punjab. Whether Napoleon would have been successful remains one of the doubtful problems of military history, along with Livy's rhetorical debate whether Alexander could have conquered the Romans. For, as events turned out, Napoleon found occupation nearer home. In 1808 began the long war in the Iberian Peninsula, in which the victor of Assaye proved that the imperial marshals were not invincible, and encouraged the nations of Europe to fresh resistance.

While the danger of a French invasion of India still appeared formidable, Lord Minto resolved to establish friendly relations with the several powers that held the keys of the north-western frontier. With this object, Malcolm was sent a second time to Persia, where his efforts were largely frustrated by another ill-advised mission which had been despatched direct from England, and of which the best-remembered result is Morier's inimitable romance, *The Adventures of Hajji Baba*. Metcalfe was sent to Lahore, where Ranjít Singh had already established himself as an independent monarch, at the head of the Sikh nationality, though with dominions much narrower than the present province of the Punjab. The treaty of amity then concluded with Metcalfe was faithfully observed by Ranjít Singh until his death in 1839; and its influence continued even through the troubled period of the First Afghán War. In nothing more than in his fidelity to his plighted word did Ranjít show himself the ablest of all the princes of India with whom the English have come in contact. At the same time, quite apart from Elphinstone's mission to Kábul, British officers were also sent to Sindh and to Baluchistán, both of which nominally formed portions of the decaying Afghán empire, together with the entire plain of the Indus from Múltán to Pesháwar, as well as the outlying mountain valley of Kashmír.

The Afghán empire had been founded sixty years earlier, on the death of the Persian conqueror Nádír Sháh, by a chief of one of the most numerous of the Afghán tribes, known to history as Ahmad Sháh Duráni. By his victory at Pánipat, in 1761, over the united armies of the Maráthá confederation, he had extended his power through Northern India as far east as Delhi, though he never claimed to supersede the effete Mughal emperors, being content to live in his native hills, happy in the possession of the crown jewels and the Kohinoor. By degrees, the Maráthás regained their influence in Hindustán proper; while the Sikhs, under Ranjít Singh, began to acquire independence in the home of their race, around the ancient cities of Lahore and Amritsar. Not very long after the death of Ahmad Sháh, the dynasty he had founded underwent the fate of all oriental monarchies, being torn asunder by fraternal rivalries, and supplanted by its own ministers and viceroys. His successor left no less than twenty-three sons, of whom three occupied the throne during the ten years between 1793 and 1803, and—more strange to relate—were all alive at this time. The first of these (fifth in order of age) was that Zemán Sháh who had, ten years previously, caused anxiety as a possible invader of Bengal; but he had now been blinded by one of his brothers, and ultimately died a British pensioner at Lúdhiána. Another, Máhmúd Sháh, after being expelled twice from Kábul, made himself independent at Herát, where he was afterwards assassinated. The third,

Sháh Shúja-úl-Múlk, passed through yet more various vicissitudes, and linked his name with English history. In 1803 he rose from the government of Peshawar to the throne of Kábul, and was still in possession when Elphinstone's embassy was sent. But his power was already tottering, and within a month after Elphinstone left him he was driven an exile into the Punjab. There he remained for nearly thirty years, until in an evil hour Lord Auckland was moved to send a British army to restore him to Kábul. The restoration was effected without much opposition; but in the winter of 1841-42, the British garrison was annihilated by a national rising of the Afgháns, and the aged Sháh Shúja was himself treacherously murdered—the last of the Duránis. The name of his dynasty survives only in the Order of the Duráni Empire, instituted in 1839, the third class of which may be worn by two veterans of the First Afghán War, Sir Henry Rawlinson and General James Abbott.

In 1808, however, so profound was English ignorance of Afghánistán [1], that the Calcutta Government may be pardoned for imagining that Sháh Shúja was firmly established on the throne, and that an alliance with him would strengthen the frontier against a possible French invasion from the direction of Persia. In this belief, Elphinstone set out from Delhi, at the head of an embassy more magnificently equipped than any that had been seen in India. He was accompanied

[1] Kábul had been visited previously by only one Englishman, George Forster, and that in disguise.

by a staff of thirteen selected English officers—
though it was a grievance with him that he was not
permitted to choose his own 'family'—and by an escort
of about 400 native troops, both cavalry and infantry.
When crossing the desert of Bikanír, this small army
required a train of 600 camels, besides thirteen elephants ; and the column, in single file, extended over
a length of two miles. As it was considered unde-
sirable to traverse the dominions of Ranjít Singh, the
route adopted lay across the sandy wastes of Rájputána, striking the Indus at Múltán. This region was
altogether outside British influence. The Rájput chiefs
were found to be engaged in active hostilities with one
another, and also subject to the inroads of the Pindárí
leader, Amir Khán. But Elphinstone was everywhere
well received, by the people as well as by the chiefs.

The only difficulty encountered was from the scarcity
of water ; for in time of war the first defensive measure
adopted was to stop up the wells. He was struck by
the knowledge frequently displayed about remote
politics. At Bikanír, the Rájá pressed upon him the
keys of the fortress, in acknowledgment of fealty to
the Company ; and one of the Sardárs (noblemen)
inquired whether the mission was not connected with
the war against the French. Baháwal Khán—the
first vassal of the Duráni Empire whom they met, and
the founder of a State which still bears his name—was
embarrassing in his hospitality. He sent hundreds
of camels laden with water to meet the embassy in
mid-desert, and he afterwards presented them with

provisions and fruits of all kinds, and also with some of the famous riding camels of the country. At Múltán, then the capital of a province under an Afghán governor, the mission halted for three weeks, in doubt as to their future movements. At last it was ascertained that the Sháh had left Kandahár for Kábul ; and accordingly they resolved to proceed northwards to Pesháwar, along the right bank of the Indus. This tract, then called Damán. but now the Deraját, is still the wildest part of India, inhabited by a mixed Afghán and Baluch population. But the mission met with no adventures, though two of the party set off on an unsuccessful attempt to scale the summit of the Takht-i-Suleimán (the Throne of Solomon), an enterprise which would not be unattended with risk at the present day.

At the salt-hills of Kálabágh, they left the plain of the Indus, and entered the glens and passes of Kohát, the only genuine bit of Afghánistán which they saw. In one day's march, the hills were so high and the valleys so deep, that the surveyors could not see the sun to take an observation at noon. It was here that Elphinstone heard the news of Wellington's victory at Vimiero, and wrote in his diary :
  'Et pulcher fugatis
   Ille dies Latio tenebris
   Qui primus alma risit adorea.'
        (HOR. *Car.* iv. 4. 39-41.)

At last, in February, 1809, four months after leaving Delhi, they arrived at Pesháwar.

Here they found Sháh Shúja residing. But at first

E

some difficulty was experienced about the manner in which they should be introduced into the august presence; for Elphinstone naturally objected to the forms which, he was told, had been submitted to by the ambassadors from Persia and Tartary.

'The ambassador to be introduced is brought into a court by two officers, who hold him firmly by the arms. On coming in sight of the King, who appears at a high window, the ambassador is made to run forward for a certain distance, when he stops for a moment and prays for the King. He is then made to run forward again, and prays once more; and after another run the King calls out *khilat* ["a dress"], which is followed by the Turkish word *getshin* ["begone"] from an officer of state, and the unfortunate ambassador is made to run out of the court, and sees no more of the King unless summoned to a private audience.'

Elphinstone's own reception was more dignified. The Sháh was clothed in a blaze of jewels, which included the far-famed Kohinoor in a bracelet above the elbow. He is described as 'a handsome man about thirty years of age, of an olive complexion, with a thick black beard. The expression of his countenance was dignified and pleasing, his voice clear, and his address princely.' Subsequently, after a private interview, Elphinstone wrote: 'It will scarcely be believed of an Eastern monarch, how much he had the manners of a gentleman, or how well he preserved his dignity, while he seemed only anxious to please.'

During the four months that the mission remained at Pesháwar, Elphinstone availed himself of his opportunities to make acquaintance with all classes of the Afgháns, whose frank, open manners he found an agreeable change from the duplicity of Marátha courtiers. He was also astonished at the knowledge that some of them had managed to acquire. Here is a description of two Muhammadans of distinction, one of whom was familiar with the details of English affairs, while the other might, under happier circumstances, have become a second Albiruni.

'Two of the most remarkable of our ordinary visitors were Mirza Gerámi Khán and Múlla Behramand. The former. the son of a Persian nobleman, had been in India, and had observed our customs with great attention and acuteness. The information he had acquired was surprising, when it is considered that the division of Europe into nations is known to few in Afghánistán, and that none of the events in our European history have been heard of even in India. I had one day been mentioning, to the amazement of some visitors, that there had not been a rebellion in our nation since 1745. and had afterwards alluded to our power at sea: when the rest of the company were gone, Mirza Gerámi told me with a smile that I had forgot the American war; and then asked seriously the reason why the insurance of ships should be raised so high by the success of French privateers when we had so manifest a superiority at sea. Múlla Behramand was a man of retired and studious habits, but really a man of genius, and of insatiable thirst for knowledge. Though well versed in metaphysics and the moral sciences known in his country, his passion was for mathematics, and he was studying Sanskrit (a language of which none of his countrymen knew the name), with a view to discover the treasures of Hindu learning.'

The country round Pesháwar, at least in early

spring, pleased Elphinstone as much as the inhabitants.

'The numerous gardens had a freshness never seen in the perpetual summer of India. Many streams ran through the plain, their banks fringed with willows and tamarisks. The orchards scattered over the country contained a profusion of plum, peach, apple, pear, quince, and pomegranate trees, which afforded a greater display of blossom than I had ever before witnessed; and the uncultivated parts of the land were covered with a thick elastic sod that perhaps never was equalled but in England. The greater part of the plain was highly cultivated, and irrigated by many water-courses and canals. Never was a spot of the same extent better peopled. From one height Lieutenant Macartney took the bearings of thirty-two villages, all within the circuit of four miles. The villages were generally large, and remarkably clean and neat, and almost all set off with trees. . . . Nothing could exceed the civility of the country people. We were often invited into gardens, and we were welcomed in every village by almost every man that saw us. They frequently entreated the gentlemen of the embassy to allow them the honour of being their hosts; and sometimes would lay hold of their bridles, and not permit them to pass until they had promised to breakfast with them on some future day, and even confirmed the promise by putting their hands between theirs.'

And this within sight of the Khaibar Pass, about whose predatory inhabitants the following story is told. An Armenian trader, who had got as far as Pesháwar on his way to Kábul, was so frightened by what he heard of the Khaibaris, that he went round by Múltán, a journey of nine weeks, instead of one of only eleven days.

At his first private interview with Sháh Shúja, Elphinstone told him that the climate, fruits, and trees of Kábul were the same as those of England, to which the Sháh replied: 'Then the two kingdoms are made by nature to be united.' The projected alliance never got much beyond these expressions of Oriental compliment, though a treaty was actually concluded and ratified by the Governor-General. But, when regarded from the retrospect of history, the whole transaction is clearly seen to have been a misunderstanding from first to last. The original plan was based upon two hypotheses, each of which turned out to be altogether erroneous. The one was that Napoleon was contemplating an invasion of India, with the assistance of Persia and Russia; the other was that Sháh Shúja was firmly seated on the throne of Afghánistán. The former assumption, whatever truth it may once have had, was being rapidly dissipated by the course of events in Europe, the news of which slowly reached Calcutta, and still more slowly penetrated to Pesháwar. Even before Elphinstone started on his mission, the Spanish insurrection had broken out, and an English army had been sent to the Peninsula. Yet more decisive was the changed attitude of the Persian court, where British influence was again predominant. The necessity, therefore, no longer existed for a defensive alliance with Kábul, which could only be useful in contingencies so remote as to be unintelligible to Oriental minds.

As regards the power of Sháh Shúja, no long stay

at Pesháwar was required to reveal the truth. Underneath the show of royal magnificence, Elphinstone quickly discovered the reality of an empty treasury, divided authority, and frequent insurrections. An old Afghán chief thus summed up to him the characteristics of his countrymen, in words that have been often quoted, and sometimes misinterpreted—for they refer, not to a foreign invader, but to a domestic despot: 'We are content with discord, we are content with alarms, we are content with blood; but we will never be content with a master.' Apart from continual rivalries between Duráni clansmen and Kazilbásh, or Persian, nobles, who formed the two parties at court, it soon became evident that Sháh Shúja's throne was already tottering. He seems to have been personally popular at Pesháwar, which he had formerly ruled as governor under Zemán Sháh; and his royal authority was still recognised at Kábul. But the province of Kashmír was in open revolt; and his brother, Máhmúd Sháh, whom he had himself supplanted, was now being set up against him at Kandahár, by a party headed by a disgraced Wazír, Fateh Khán Barakzái, from whom the present Amír is descended.

Therefore, while Elphinstone's instructions were to conclude a defensive alliance against the French, the main object of Sháh Shúja was to obtain pecuniary and military assistance against his own revolted subjects, which it was beyond Elphinstone's power to grant. At one time he suggested the advisability of purchasing from the Sháh his nominal suzerainty over Sind; for he always seems to have been impressed with the danger of an invasion from that quarter. And when it was too late, he received authority from the Governor-General to offer £300,000, 'if morally assured of corresponding benefit to the British interests.' As a matter of fact, all that he accomplished, after tedious negotiations with the Ministers and their subordinate agents, was the conclusion of a colourless treaty, by which the English undertook to assist Sháh Shújá with money, in case of a joint invasion of Afghánistán by France and Persia; while Sháh Shújá bound himself to resist such a confederacy, and to exclude all Frenchmen from his dominions for ever.

This treaty was signed at Pesháwar on the 19th of April, and formally ratified at Calcutta by Lord Minto on the 14th of June, 1809. But between these two dates Sháh Shújá's circumstances had greatly altered; and Elphinstone had found it prudent to quit Pesháwar and cross the Indus. On the 23rd of April, only four days after the conclusion of the treaty, intelligence reached Pesháwar that the army sent to reconquer Kashmír had been totally routed; and at the same time came the confirmation of a previous report that Máhmúd Sháh had occupied Kábul. These two disasters created something like a panic in Pesháwar, and caused Elphinstone's position to be no longer tenable. He waited on, however, while the defeated soldiers came straggling back from Kashmír, which gave him the opportunity of seeing Akrám Khán, the bravest and most influential of the Duráni generals. Sháh Shúja himself still professed to keep up heart, and was encouraged by the prayers of the people of Pesháwar, ' to whom his moderation and justice had greatly endeared him.' On the 4th of June the escort was exercised in honour of King George's birthday. Akrám Khán and other chiefs who were present greatly admired the display, and said: 'If the Duránis had such discipline, they would beat everything.' On the same day Elphinstone recorded in his diary: ' I fear Sháh Shúja must fall; but (as the Musalmáns say) God is powerful, and there is no place where He shows his power with more irregularity than here. I have had a letter from Máhmúd Sháh. I declined replying, but declared the neutrality of my Government.'

It is to the credit of Sháh Shúja that his courteous treatment of the mission never altered. When he had at length resolved to risk his future on the issue of one more battle, he bade a hearty farewell to Elphinstone in his camp, saying ' that we must be unaccustomed to so unsettled a government as his was at present; and that although he parted with us with reluctance, he was unwilling to expose us to the inconvenience of a campaign, and he therefore wished us to retire to some place on the frontier, from which we could either join him or return to India, as suited our convenience.' Accordingly, on the 14th of June, 1809, the mission left Pesháwar, proceeding first to the passage over the Indus at Attock, and then to Hassan Abdál. Here Elphinstone received a letter of recall from the Governor-General. Here also he was overtaken by the harem of Sháh Shúja, who brought the news of another crushing defeat: that Akrám Khán had been killed, fighting bravely, and that the Sháh himself was a fugitive on the mountains. The vicissitudes of the Afghán monarchy were illustrated by a visit to the blind exile, Zemán Sháh, who received them with dignity, and told sad stories of the deaths of kings, from Tamerlane downwards.

The mission was now within Sikh territory. They halted for some time at Ráwal Pindi, before they could obtain permission from Ranjít Singh to advance. The Sikhs did not create a favourable impression on Elphinstone: he thought them unmannerly and given up to drunkenness. The only notable incident in the long march across the Punjab was a visit to the Buddhist Tope of Mánikyála, of which Elphinstone presents a plate in his book, and in the architecture of which he was the first to trace Greek influence. It is perhaps worthy of mention that he always gives their Greek names to the Five Rivers of the Punjab. At Lúdhiána he found himself in a British cantonment. Thence he proceeded leisurely to Delhi, which he reached in September, the whole journey from Pesháwar having taken three months. The mission was not broken up until the following June (1810), when Elphinstone was ordered to Calcutta. Indeed, so late as April, 1810, there seems to have been some notion of reopening diplomatic relations with Kábul.

The intermediate time was occupied in preparing the official report of the mission, different branches of inquiry being assigned to the several officers. Elphinstone himself undertook the government and the manners of the people, which form the subject of his later published book. While at Peshawar it was thought imprudent to arouse suspicions by pressing researches too closely; and most of the material was acquired subsequently, from Afgháns and other natives of countries beyond the frontier who accompanied the mission on its return to India, or who were met with in Delhi and its neighbourhood. Special visits of investigation were also paid to the great fair at Hardwár, and to the Afghán colony of Rohilkhand. The Report was finally transmitted to Government at the end of 1810, when Elphinstone had arrived at Calcutta[1]. In a letter of about the same date, he wrote to his sister: 'I have been two years and a half away, in which time I have gone five thousand miles.'

[1] It has never been printed, and is understood to be still buried among the records of the India Office.

CHAPTER VII

RESIDENT AT POONA

1811—1817

SHORTLY after his arrival at Calcutta, Elphinstone was appointed to be Resident at Poona—a post which seems to have been kept open for him during his absence. The failure of the Kábul embassy had quenched his ambition; and he now looked forward only to a few years of comparative repose before he could retire from Indian service on a competency. But, as it turned out, he was entering upon the final stage of his career, when his conduct of affairs at a critical juncture was destined to win for him a place in history, and to transform him henceforth from a diplomatist into an administrator.

He spent several months at Calcutta before starting for Poona, concluding the official report of his mission and enjoying the company of his early friends, Strachey and Adam. This time he went by sea, direct to Bombay. The voyage was accomplished in an Arab coasting-vessel, owned by a merchant from the Persian Gulf, and manned by a miscellaneous crew of natives. Including the passengers, there were people on board who could speak twenty-five languages. Among them was Henry Martyn, the missionary, bound on the expedition to Persia from which he was fated never to return. Elphinstone found him a far better companion than he had reckoned on, though his expectations were high. He describes him as 'an excellent scholar, and one of the mildest, cheerfullest, and pleasantest men I ever saw. He is extremely religious, and disputes about the faith with the Nakhoda [the captain of the vessel, an Abyssinian slave]; but talks on all subjects sacred and profane, and laughs and makes others laugh as heartily as he could do if he were an infidel.'

The vessel touched at Ceylon, and again at Goa. Here they went ashore and visited the churches, though they were not admitted within the buildings of the Inquisition. At Bombay, Elphinstone became the guest of Malcolm, who introduced him to Sir James Mackintosh, the Recorder. The latter wrote of him in his diary: 'He has a very fine understanding, with the greatest modesty and simplicity of character.' It was from Mackintosh that he received the stimulus to write his published work on Afghánistán. Another friend that he made on this occasion was William Erskine, son-in-law of Mackintosh, and the literary executor of the ill-fated Dr. Leyden. Elphinstone's deeper Oriental studies and his subsequent interest in jurisprudence were alike due to Erskine's inspiration; and the intimate intercourse between them continued, in England, until Erskine's death.

Elphinstone reached Poona in May, 1811, having

spent about five months on the journey. He found but little changed in the past nine years. Bájí Ráo was still Peshwa, strengthened in his position by the long peace, but secretly chafing at the restraints of a subsidiary alliance. The country was slowly recovering from the famine of 1803—the most severe ever known in the Deccan—which had been caused by the ravages of Holkar's army in the previous year. The Peshwa had taken advantage of British support to tighten the reins of his authority over numerous vassal chiefs, who divided among themselves almost half his dominions, and at the same time to accumulate a reserve of treasure against any emergency.

The first political question that Elphinstone took up was one that had been too long allowed to remain unsettled. By the Treaty of Bassein, the Peshwa was not only guaranteed against external enemies; it was also provided that the subsidiary force should be employed 'for the overcoming and chastising of rebels.' By 'rebels' the Peshwa understood all those within the limits of his territory who would not submit to his own absolute rule. In other words, he claimed to reduce to the position of subjects the numerous class of Jagírdárs, who derived their authority from his predecessors, or, in some cases, from old grants by the Mughal Emperors. General Arthur Wellesley had attempted to intervene between the Peshwa and the Jagírdárs, shortly after the conclusion of the Second Maráthá War; and Strachey had been deputed on an unsuccessful mission to establish a compromise on the spot. Afterwards, the difficulty was allowed to smoulder, in accordance with the policy of non-intervention that followed Lord Wellesley's departure from India, until at last Elphinstone planned a final settlement, for the execution of which he obtained the sanction of Lord Minto. This settlement of the Southern Maráthá country has continued almost unaltered to the present day.

The Rájá of Sátára, the lineal heir of Sivají, the founder of the Marátha Empire, did not come within the scheme. For several generations the Rájás of Sátára had dwelt in complete obscurity at their capital, as *rois fainéants,* leaving all authority in the hands of successive Peshwas, who originally acquired power as their Bráhman ministers or Mayors of the Palace. To touch the Rájá of Sátára at this time would have been to disturb the fountain from which Bájí Ráo derived his own dignity. But the Rájá of Kolhápur, another descendant of the stock of Sivají, gave much trouble. It was decided to recognise him as an independent sovereign; but he would not consent to the limits fixed for his State. Ultimately, after troops had been moved against him, a treaty was signed by which he surrendered to the Presidency of Bombay the strong fort and harbour of Malwán in the Konkan, which had long been a nest of pirates, in consideration of the British Government foregoing an old debt of £50,000. At the same time the State of Sáwantwári was also deprived of its seaboard.

The future status of the Jagírdárs proper was

settled without much opposition, owing to the overwhelming military force which Elphinstone was able to throw into their country in the middle of the rainy season. He had at his disposal no less than twenty battalions of infantry and four regiments of cavalry, besides some thousands of irregular horse from Mysore and the Nizam. Overawed by this display, the Jagírdárs, without exception, submitted to the terms which Strachey had offered them in vain six years previously, and to which Elphinstone now won the reluctant consent of the Peshwa. By these terms they were confirmed in their hereditary *jagírs*, though some of them were deprived of acquisitions made during the recent anarchy; the claim of the Peshwa to military and other services from them was recognised; while they were guaranteed against any fresh exactions by a pledge of security from the British Government.

Elphinstone thoroughly enjoyed taking part in this bloodless campaign during the months of July and August, 1812. Here is an extract from his diary, under date August 6:

'Business went on with great rapidity, when it was no longer embarrassed by the necessity of consulting the Peshwa. I required, however, to move the force before I could bring in the Jagírdárs. They are all in now, and everything may be said to be settled; but the troops must keep the field till all is quite secure. I had many pleasant little parties of officers. We went out three or four days to hunt hogs, though we were not always successful.

'We marched to-day at day-break, and saw nothing remarkable on the way but a *khitmatgár* [butler] of Chimnají Appa, who was rolling from Poona to Pandarpur, in performance of a vow he had made for a child. He had been a month at it, and has become so expert that he went on smoothly and without pausing, and kept rolling evenly along the middle of the road, over stones and everything. He travelled at the rate of two koss a day.'

When the business of the Jagírdárs had been settled, Elphinstone set to work with renewed energy on his book about Kábul. As already mentioned, the first impulse to authorship seems to have come from Sir James Mackintosh, who wrote letters to hold him to his promise. Scarcely less stimulating was a visit from Malcolm, who was himself engaged at this time upon his *History of Persia*. Erskine helped him with his Oriental learning and with the loan of MSS.; and his old friend Jenkins subjected his first draft to a rigorous revision.

At first he thought only of publishing his official report, entitled, 'An Account of the Nations subject to the King of Caubul, with some Information regarding the Neighbouring States.' But the task grew under his hands, until at last it assumed a very different form. Even regarding the Report he stated that, owing to the jealousy of the Afghán Government, most of the information was gathered from natives of Afghánistán after the mission had left the country. So now he writes that

'I have generally spent the time I could spare from business and other avocations in interrogating Afgháns respecting their particular tribes and connexions; and though I have acquired a knowledge of the whole kingdom and an intimacy with details which I by no means possessed before, I have multiplied my materials, and increased the difficulty of digesting and arranging them.'

The actual work of composition seems to have been chiefly accomplished during the cold season of 1813-14, when Elphinstone estimated that he ought to be able to spare four hours a day for the purpose. Undoubtedly he derived great benefit from it. Not only did it win for him a literary reputation in England, but it served to concentrate his studies and to give him greater confidence in his own powers. He despatched the MS. to England in June 1814, when he calculated that, under the most favourable circumstances, he could not receive a review of it for eighteen months. Of course he had no opportunity of correcting the proofs. The book was published by Messrs. Longmans & Co., in 1815, in a magnificent quarto, with map and coloured engravings, under the title *An Account of the Kingdom of Caubul and its Dependencies in Persia, Tartary, and India*. A second and revised edition (1839), in two volumes octavo, is now more commonly met with. The success of the book was immediate. Malcolm, who was then at home at the height of his fame, went about praising it everywhere; and Sir James Mackintosh reviewed it in the *Edinburgh Review*. Despite the volumes of literature that have since been published about Afghánistán, Elphinstone still remains the standard authority. He is quoted with respect by M. James Darmesteter, in his *Chants Populaires des Afghans*, a work of equal learning and perspicuity, which has once and for all determined the affinities of the Pushtu language.

This period was perhaps the happiest of Elphinstone's life. Bombay was near enough to bring a constant succession of visitors, among whom we hear of several ladies, especially Lady Hood, who had lately seen all his friends in England. He delighted in taking them on little tours through the Deccan, to visit old ruins or romantic scenery. Nor was his general reading intermitted. On his voyage round from Calcutta he had carried with him Polybius and Scott's *Dryden*. Shortly afterwards he took up Corneille and Racine, both of whom he admired much —the latter most. In company with Lady Hood, he read Dante. An habitual fellow-student was found in a young doctor, named Jeffreys, with whom he went through a regular course of Greek, beginning with the Port Royal Grammar. They also read together Lucan and Lucretius. He re-read Gibbon's Autobiography, with the object of encouraging himself for his own work on Afghánistán. Sir George Staunton's Account of Lord Macartney's Embassy to China in 1792 drew from him an interesting comment on the political condition of the Chinese as compared with the Hindus. Later, he returned to this subject, which seems to have possessed the same fascination for him that the religious development of

China has for the most philosophical of our living Indian statesmen.

The following extracts from Elphinstone's diary and letters at this time are quoted without any exact regard for chronology. His plan of life was to ride ten to twenty miles in the morning, to do the *kasrat* (a bodily exercise), apply to public business and private correspondence from about ten to two, then lunch on a few sandwiches and figs and a glass of water, after which a siesta of half an hour.

'I then begin to read or examine people about the Afgháns. In the evening I used to drive out: I now do the *kasrat* a second time. I dine on a few potatoes and one or two glasses of claret and water, and then, after reading for some time, go to sleep at eleven.'

Here is a story of Marátha rapine, told in connexion with the town of Sindur, not far from Násik:

'Its ruin was completed by the dissension which prevailed among the Maráthás after the present Peshwa's accession. Muhammad Khán made it long his headquarters, and ransacked every hole and corner in it. Even my fat, lazy, luxurious *munshi* [interpreter] was a soldier in those troublous times, and had the plunder of the place assigned for the pay of himself and three hundred horse he had in the service of Jube, then in rebellion against Sindia. He came, forced the gate without resistance, seized a Kákar and other people of property, and showed them no mercy till they had ransomed themselves. The *munshi* got 8000 or 9000 rupees for his own share, I believe.'

His recognition of the true methods of archaeological

research is shown in one of his earliest letters to
Erskine :

'Soon after my return to this place [Poona] from Bombay
I sent a painter to Kárlí to copy the inscriptions on the
caves. I also sent a Bráhman writer to compare the copies
with the original inscriptions, and serve as a check on the
painter's fancy. . . . I this day send them to you by a cooly.
I hope you will do something towards deciphering them.
This seems an unreasonable expectation; but I am led to it
by the reports I have heard of your success in discovering
the history of some other caves, which I suppose could only
be done by means of the inscriptions. I have no doubt you
will be struck by the resemblance between them and the
inscriptions copied from the pillars of Delhi and Allahábád,
published in the seventh volume of the *Asiatick Researches*,
but, on comparison, the characters will not be found the
same.'

Finally, here is an epitaph on Sir Barry Close, his
first master in Oriental diplomacy, composed in a
style that recalls the panegyric of Agricola by
Tacitus :

'We have heard of the death of Sir Barry Close. I doubt
whether such an assemblage of manly virtues remains behind
him. A strong and hardy frame, a clear head and vigorous
understanding, fixed principles, unshaken courage, contempt
for pomp and pleasure, entire devotion to the public service,
joined to the utmost modesty and simplicity, formed the
character of Sir Barry Close—a character such as one would
rather think imagined in ancient Rome than met with in
our own age and nation.'

But we must now return to public affairs, which
henceforth absorbed all Elphinstone's attention. Lord

Moira (better known as the Marquis of Hastings) succeeded Lord Minto in 1812, and under his rule a new era of war was inaugurated. The hollow peace patched up by Sir George Barlow with the Maráthá powers had, indeed, lasted longer than its critics anticipated. The regular forces of the Maráthás were no longer formidable, while the British army seems to have maintained a high standard both of numbers and efficiency. The real trouble was the increase in strength and audacity of the Pindárís, whom the Marátha Chiefs were alike unable and unwilling to restrain, and whom the English could not deal with except at the risk of provoking a general conflagration. Encouraged by their immunity, some of the Pindárí leaders began to form regular armies of horse, foot, and artillery, and to found petty principalities for themselves. All Central India and Rájputána was in a state of chronic anarchy, the effects of which spread throughout the Deccan; while Pindárí raids occasionally extended as far south as the maritime districts of the Karnatik [1]. It had long been clear to all that a 'Pindárí hunt,' to adopt Elphinstone's phrase, had become a necessity, if the British claim to paramount power was to have any meaning. The sole subject of doubt was whether the great Marátha Chiefs would remain quiet while their old auxiliaries

[1] In one raid to the Coromandel coast, it is reported that, in the course of ten days, 389 villages were plundered and many of them burnt; that 182 persons were put to death, 500 wounded, and 3600 subjected to torture; and that the loss of property exceeded £250,000.

were being extirpated. While matters were in this unsettled condition, the repeated incursions of the Gúrkhas on the northern frontier of Hindustan compelled Lord Hastings to engage in a prolonged war with a brave and active foe amid the lower slopes of the Himálayas. When this was finished, it was well understood that the Pindárí question would be taken up in earnest.

To some extent we have anticipated events, for the first troubles that befell Elphinstone had nothing to do with the Pindárí question, except in so far as the general uneasiness of all the Marátha Chiefs had its origin in dread of the British designs.

After the settlement with the Southern Jagírdárs already described, the Peshwa proceeded to strengthen his personal power by every means. As a counterbalance to the feudal militia now placed under his authority, he raised a new force commanded by British officers, but independent of the subsidiary contingent, which was nominally intended for the protection of the frontier against the Pindárís. Of this force, generally called 'the Brigade,' the command was given to Major Ford. Confusion in military organisation was equalled by confusion in diplomatic relations. The great Marátha Chiefs—such as Sindia, Holkar, the Bhonsla Rájá of Nágpur, and the Gáekwár of Baroda—and also the Nizam still continued to maintain representatives at Poona, for the discussion of disputes relating to boundaries or tribute, which were never settled. An active correspondence was carried on between the several courts by means of a regular staff of messengers. In short, the Peshwa was attempting to break loose from the restraints of the subsidiary system; and the Resident was not eager to interfere with him, relying upon his own complete knowledge of all that was going on, and trusting to the timidity of Bájí Ráo's nature to avoid an outbreak. He thus describes him in a despatch of about this date, in language that again suggests reminiscences of Tacitus:

'The character of His Highness the Peshwa has always perplexed those who have been interested in discovering his sentiments or calculating on his conduct. This is partly owing to the inconsistency of many of his inclinations with his ruling passion of fear, and partly to the deep dissimulation which enables him to conceal his real feelings and intentions, and to display others which are foreign to his mind. If he were less deficient in courage, he would be ambitious, imperious, inflexible, and persevering; and his active propensities would probably overcome his love of ease and pleasure, which are now so strong, from their alliance with his timidity. As it is, he is eager for power, though he wants the boldness necessary to acquire it, and is tenacious of authority, though too indolent to exercise it. Even his indolence is broken in on by his habits of suspicion and vigilance, and there is no part of his character that is to be found unmixed and entire. His love of consequence makes him fond of the company of low dependants, where he can enjoy his superiority unresisted. With them he is haughty and overbearing, and even with others he is proud and lofty on some occasions; but when it suits his purposes, there is no meanness to which he will not descend. Though capricious and changeable in his humours, he is steady in his serious designs. Concession encourages him to persevere, and opposition only increases his obstinacy, unless it operates on his fears. He is vindictive in the extreme; he never forgets an injury, and spares no machinations to ruin the object of his resentment. These arts, indeed, cost him little; for, to his habitual insincerity he joins a talent for insinuation, and a natural love of intrigue and artifice. . . .

'To balance his vices, it must be admitted that the Peshwa is by no means deficient in abilities; that he is scrupulously just in pecuniary transactions; humane, when not actuated by fear or revenge; frugal, but not parsimonious in his expenses; and at once courteous and dignified in his manners.

'Some other parts of the Peshwa's character must be mentioned, though they do not affect his public conduct. He is a slave to superstition: half his life is spent in fasts, prayers, and pilgrimages. A large portion of his revenue is consumed in magical practices, and his life is disturbed by his attention to prodigies and omens. His superstition imposes no restraint upon his pleasures, and the greater part of his time that is not occupied by religion is devoted to vicious indulgences. Though he affects great purity in his own person, scarcely a day passes that he does not spend some hours with his favourites in large assemblies of women. when he enjoys the coarsest buffoonery, and witnesses most disgusting scenes of debauchery.'

Such is the portrait, drawn by a master hand, of one who is perhaps best remembered by Englishmen as the adoptive father of Ná̃ná Sáhib. The element of daring, in which his own character was deficient, was supplied by one of his favourites, Trimbakjí Dánglia, whom about this time he raised from menial service to the rank of Minister. This man had first recommended himself by his readiness in farming the revenue of certain districts at a higher rate than any one else would offer, of course indemnifying himself by extortion ; and he afterwards made his position secure by the boldness with which he undertook to execute the designs of his master. Elphinstone thought it best to raise no objection to the sudden elevation of Trimbakjí, apparently in the confidence that the concealed intrigues would now be brought to an open head, and thus more easily defeated. He was certainly under no illusion with regard to Trimbakjí's character.

'He is so absolutely illiterate as not to have learned to read, and his manners and understanding are such as might be expected from the class to which he belongs. He is entirely ignorant of the state of India, of the comparative importance of his master's State, and of its relation to the British Government as fixed by treaty. To this must be added that he bears a bad character, even among the Maráthás, for falsehood and want of faith.'

The expected crisis was not long delayed ; nor was Elphinstone wanting in the energy to deal with it. In order to settle a long-standing difference about territory, the Gáekwár of Baroda had sent an agent, named Gangadhar Shástrí, to the court of the Peshwa. The Shástrí, who was himself a Poona Bráhman, entertained not unjustifiable fears for his personal safety, and accordingly sought and obtained a safe-conduct from the British Government. After in-

effectual negotiations, the Peshwa attempted to win
over the envoy's allegiance, by promising one of his
own daughters in marriage to his son. When this
failed, the Shástrí was invited on a visit of devotion
to Pandharpur, and there barbarously murdered in
the street of the town. The actual motives for this
crime remain obscure; but there can be little doubt
that Trimbakjí was the instigator of it: at any rate,
he took no steps to investigate the circumstances,
though they passed almost under his eyes.

Elphinstone, who happened at the time to be exploring the caves of Ellora, did not hesitate to act at
once on his own responsibility, without waiting for
the instructions of the Governor-General. He collected the evidence of the Shástrí's surviving attendants, and addressed a forcible letter to the Peshwa,
expressing his conviction of Trimbakjí's guilt, and
demanding his surrender.

'A foreign ambassador has been murdered in the midst
of your Highness's court: a Bráhman has been massacred
almost in the temple, during one of the great solemnities of
your religion. And I must not conceal from your Highness
that the impunity of the perpetrators of this enormity has
led to imputations not to be thought of against your
Highness's government.

The Peshwa sent a succession of dilatory messages,
declined to grant Elphinstone an audience, shut himself up in his palace, strengthened his guard, and
summoned to Poona additional troops, to the number
of 18,000 men. Elphinstone, who had now obtained

the approval of the Marquis of Hastings to his course of action, replied by counter demonstrations. The remaining members of the Baroda mission were invited to encamp in the neighbourhood of the Residency; the garrison of British troops, and the newly raised brigade under Major Ford, were both placed on the alert; while the subsidiary force was brought back from the frontier to their cantonments at Sirur, and subsequently moved nearer to Poona. These military movements convinced the Peshwa that Elphinstone was in earnest. After more tedious negotiations, he at last consented to surrender Trimbakjí to a detachment of Major Ford's brigade, under an assurance that his life would be spared, and that no further inquiry would be made into the circumstances of the crime. Two other prominent accessories were at the same time given up to the government of the Gáekwár. The date of the surrender was the 15th September, 1815, just two months after the murder.

But the affair of Trimbakjí was not so easily settled. In truth, it led directly to the series of events which cost the Peshwa his throne. Elphinstone had recommended Allahábád or Chunár, within the Bengal Presidency, for Trimbakjí's imprisonment. The place chosen was the fort of Thána, in the island of Salsette, almost under the eyes of the Bombay Government. For additional security, the guard placed over him was composed of European soldiers. Everything conspired to facilitate the plot for his escape. A Maráthá groom took service with an officer of the garrison, and while daily leading his horse under the windows of the fort, used to sing to the prisoner, in the hearing of the English sentry, whatever intelligence he wished to convey. When all was ready, a hole was dug through the wall; and after less than a year's confinement, Trimbakjí found himself again free, and safe from pursuit among the mountains of the Western Gháts. A Marátha ballad, which is still sung by wandering bards, tells, with additions, this romantic story, which combines incidents from the escape of Richard the First with incidents from border legend.

During the period of Trimbakjí's imprisonment, we hear little of politics, but much about literature, something about sport, and for the first time allusions to a hope of returning home overland, and a tour through Greece on the way, which was not to be realised for twelve years longer. Elphinstone calculated that five years' service was yet required before he could retire on £1500 a year, and then he would be forty-two years of age—'too old to set up a wife and family, and likewise too old to mix in society, so as to be able to get on without them. . . . As to action or distinction that is gone long ago.' Yet both were to come within twelve months.

In a letter to Strachey, dated February, 1816, Elphinstone thus describes his mode of life during this brief interlude of tranquillity.

'I used to be constantly employed in resisting the encroachments and intrigues of the former Minister [Trimbakjí]; and now I have time to read Cicero till twelve every day, and Herodotus with Jeffreys from six o'clock till dinner-time. I hope my godson will know more Greek at ten than I do after twenty years' reading of it, off and on. We have a hog-hunt that goes out every second Wednesday, in the evening, to some place from ten to twenty miles off, hunts on Thursday, returning on Friday to breakfast. We hog-hunt till two, then "tiff," and hawk or course till dusk.... We do not throw our spears in the old way, but poke with spears longer than the common ones, and never part with them. This, with officers from camp to breakfast and dinner (now and then), and occasional visitors from Bombay or Sirur, makes up our life, which is equally exempt from gaiety and melancholy.'

A different style is shown in a letter to his aunt, Lady Keith:

'I am writing in a garden of trees, some of which have no names in English, and others are among the rarest in your greenhouses. My room is filled with the smoke of incense, burned before a Hindu god not ten yards from my house, where troops of women come, with music playing before them, to hang up garlands, to sacrifice sheep, and to cut off their own hair, which they have vowed to the divinity. In the same garden there is a very ancient ruined tomb of a Muhammadan female saint, which is a place of such sanctity that an oath taken in it is reckoned sacred, even among the faithless people. I have just heard loud lamentations over a dead body; and I now see a funeral pyre kindling on the banks of a river close at hand, where I have before seen the living consumed with the dead. The mourners are sitting in silence on the ground, looking on till it be time to gather up the ashes of their friend. Two large elephants are wallowing in the water at no great distance; and on the road that crosses the river are buffaloes, camels, horsemen with long spears and loose drapery, and foot-passengers male and female, in dresses of all sorts and colours. At this moment a procession is passing of Muhammadans dressed like Arabs, performing a frantic dance, and flourishing their drawn swords in honour of the sons of Ali, of whose martyrdom this is the anniversary. The whole town is ringing with drumming, trumpeting, and shouting, occasioned by the same festival. And to make the whole still more unlike England, the country round is laid waste by a body of predatory horse, who have made an inroad from beyond the Narbadá, and have driven the inhabitants of the neighbouring villages in on the capital.'

The re-appearance of Trimbakjí brought anxieties to Elphinstone, and encouragement to the Peshwa in his now scarcely concealed plans of hostility to the English. Trimbakjí escaped in September 1816, but nothing certain was known about his movements until the following January. Then news began to reach Elphinstone that bands of horse and foot were assembling at a temple of Mahádeo (the national deity of the Maráthás), in the mountains somewhere between Narsinghpur and Purandhar. He also received secret information that the Peshwa was in constant correspondence, not only with Trimbakjí, but also with the other Marátha courts, who were all alike rendered uneasy by the increasing preparations for a Pindárí war.

Elphinstone had no reason now to complain of the inefficiency of his intelligence department, under the charge of Captain (afterwards Major-General) Briggs. who thus describes the system:

'My acquaintance with the languages induced Mr. Elphinstone at an early period to employ me in making translations of the numerous *akhbárs* [despatches] he was at that time in the habit of receiving from the native courts of India, where he had established intelligencers; and his own previous acquaintance with the Ministers while Resident at Nagpur made him familiar with their characters and connexions. At the time I speak of, we had regular postal communication with the several capitals of these Chiefs; and as the whole of that department was under our own postmaster at Poona, it was not difficult in a great degree to depend on their reports, which were occasionally checked by sending a confidential agent along each line, under the plea of paying these intelligencers, and to report circumstantially the actual state of affairs. Baji Rao's foreign communications were made either by means of camel *harkáras* [messengers], or by special foot-messengers, whose progress was detected by the small javelins the latter carried, every court having them painted differently, to enable them to command any necessary aid they might require on their route. This answered as a sort of livery, but was recognised only by the officials of the several princes. Similar javelins were used by the messengers of the bankers of the different cities in the Native States, but they were for the most part painted in one colour. In this way we at Poona obtained instant information of the entry of any of the messengers of foreign courts that might pass our postal stations, and were enabled to be on the lookout for their arrival, as well as to trace the direction of any despatch by the Peshwa.'

The system was even yet more widely-reaching than here described. In a despatch to the Governor-

General, dated the 11th of March, 1817[1], Elphinstone gives details of the movements of Trimbakjí during the two previous months. From the 15th to the 29th of January, the news-writer at Narsinghpur sent no less than six different letters, first mentioning rumours, and finally specifying the number and the disposition of Trimbakjí's followers. Early in February, news-writers at Poona began to communicate intelligence similar to that received from Narsinghpur; and by the middle of the month full confirmation of it was received from two Bráhmans, who were sent separately to the temple of Mahádeo to collect information. On the 24th of February, a person of some consequence, long connected with the British Government, brought to Elphinstone the chief of a village who had actually enlisted in Trimbakjí's service with twenty horse. On the 1st of March, the Narsinghpur writer sends accounts of more gatherings. He specifies as usual the villages where they are quartered, and in many cases the names of the commanders. On the 2nd, he writes that 213,000 rupees have been sent from Pandharpur in the night to Trimbakjí. He mentions names of persons concerned in sending the money, and the spot where a party of horse was stationed for the purpose of furnishing an escort. About the beginning of this month a peasant came in to report that troops were quartered in his village. *Harkáras* were sent back with this man, who showed them the horses; while

[1] See Forrest's *Selections*, p. 144, where the year is incorrectly given as 1815.

another party of horse passed them, travelling secretly and by night. On the 7th of March, a person came to a broker employed to collect intelligence, and asked him to exchange some gold coin. By welldirected inquiries, the broker discovered that the gold had been issued by Trimbakjí to a Pathán chief who had enlisted with him, and whose servant the person offering the money was.

Fortified by all this consentient information, Elphinstone repeatedly addressed remonstrances to the Peshwa, calling upon him to put down the incipient insurrection, and to arrest Trimbakjí as a rebel against his own authority. The Peshwa first denied that any hostile forces were assembled, then sent out a detachment of his own troops under a native officer who did nothing, and finally assumed an attitude of obstinate resistance to all proposals.

Elphinstone was now firmly persuaded, not only that the Peshwa was supporting Trimbakjí's armed movement, but also that his intrigues with other native courts had reached a head. Accordingly, the British troops and Major Ford's brigade were a second time placed on the alert, the subsidiary force was again moved from the frontier towards the capital, and requisitions for military support were sent to the officers commanding on the borders of Haidarábád and Mysore. Meanwhile, Elphinstone was unwilling to precipitate matters until he should receive instructions from Calcutta in reply to his despatch of the 15th of March. The speed of postal communications at this time is evidenced by the fact that these instructions were sent off on the 7th of April; though, owing to disturbances in Orissa, they did not reach Poona until the 10th of May.

In the meantime, Elphinstone had been compelled to act on his own responsibility. On the last day of March, he wrote in his diary:

'The Peshwa submitted yesterday, and agreed to dismiss his troops, dismantle his garrisons, and wait the Governor-General's decision, which I have told him would be more or less severe in proportion to the sincerity with which he acts against the rebels. I do not much think his Highness is at all sincere. Even if he is, we may have a row still.'

The 'row' nearly came that very night. For on the evening of the 31st of March, while Elphinstone was playing a round game of cards with several ladies, Captain Briggs interrupted him with news that the streets of Poona were full of armed men; that the gun-cattle had arrived an hour before; and that the Peshwa was in full *darbár* (council), discussing with his nobles the question of immediate war. Though the Residency itself was inadequately guarded, the idea was for a short time entertained of attacking the city at once from the cantonment. Elphinstone, however, in pursuance of his fixed policy, decided to wait till the morning; while the Peshwa, for his part, was unable to summon up enough courage to give the signal for attack.

The whole of April passed without any outbreak, being consumed in futile negotiations, and in bringing up reinforcements on both sides. At last, on the 6th of May, when Elphinstone ascertained that the post from Calcutta had been intercepted, he resolved to issue an ultimatum. The night before he had had a final interview with the Peshwa, who was collected, conciliatory, and able, but would not pledge himself to give up Trimbakjí.

'I thought it possible that, in these extremities, he might seize me for a hostage and carry me off to Singarh; but he seemed not to have the most distant thought that way. . . . With all his crimes and all his perfidy, I shall be sorry if Bájí Ráo throws away his sovereignty.'

The ultimatum took the form of a written demand for the immediate cession of the three historic hill-fortresses of Purandhar, Ráigarh, and Singhgarh, as securities for the seizure of Trimbakjí within one month. If the forts were not handed over within twenty-four hours, then hostilities would begin. After the usual shuffling, and when the troops, under the command of General Smith, had already closed every approach to the city, the Peshwa at last sent orders that the fortresses should be surrendered. Four days later the delayed instructions of the Governor-General arrived, imposing yet more severe terms. These were that the Peshwa should sign a new treaty, undertaking to maintain no envoys at foreign courts, and to receive none at Poona; renouncing all claim to the titular headship of the Marátha empire, and acknowledging his entire dependence upon the British Government. He was further required to surrender territory for the maintenance of the subsidiary force, and to acknowledge on the face of the treaty his belief in Trimbakjí's guilt. These humiliating conditions were to be insisted on only in the event of the Peshwa's taking no active measures for the arrest of Trimbakji. As the Peshwa continued to do nothing, and even renewed his warlike preparations, Elphinstone was compelled to force the treaty upon him. It was signed on the 13th of June, 1817; but both parties were well aware that its sanction depended, not upon the signature of the Peshwa, but upon the military superiority of the British. As a matter of fact, Trimbakjí seems never to have been surrendered for the second time: in October of this year we hear of him as again in arms. He was finally captured at the end of the Third Marátha War, and confined as a State prisoner at Chunár, on the Ganges. There he was visited in 1824 by Bishop Heber, who thus versifies the song of the Marátha groom [1]:

> 'Behind the bush the bowmen hide,
>   The horse beneath the tree:
> Where shall I find a knight will ride
>   The jungle paths with me?
> There are five and fifty coursers there,
>   And four and fifty men:
> When the fifty-fifth shall mount his steed,
>   The Deccan thrives again!'

[1] *Journal*, i. 585.

CHAPTER VIII

THE THIRD MARÁTHÁ WAR

1817—1818

THE future course of events at Poona forms a chapter in the history of what is commonly known as the Third Marátha War. Arising out of the combined operations for the suppression of the Pindárís, this war owes its importance to the part played by the Peshwa, the Rájá of Nágpur, and Holkar. Its conclusion brought about the final downfall of the Marátha confederacy, which never again united against the British; the augmentation of the Bombay Presidency almost to its present dimensions; and the pacification of Central India. The heroes of the fighting were Malcolm, Elphinstone, and Munro.

During the whole of the year 1817, the Marquis of Hastings was engaged in making preparations for the coming war. An army, stronger in numbers than had ever before been collected in British India[1], was gradually concentrated under the Commander-in-Chief, Sir Thomas Hislop. Malcolm received a mission to visit all the courts of India, to consult with

[1] The total force put into the field, including auxiliaries, amounted to 116,000 men, with 300 guns.

the Residents, and to re-assure the minds of the princes. He also received—what he valued more highly—the rank of Brigadier-General, with a promise that he should accompany the most advanced force in action. And he wrote to his wife: 'From the Governor-General down to the lowest black or white, red or brown, clothed or naked, all appear happy at my advancement.'

This was by no means such a happy time for Elphinstone, though in reality it was but the dark hour before the dawn of his brightest day. He was evidently not quite satisfied with the new treaty which it had been his duty to impose on the Peshwa. Perhaps for this reason, perhaps because he thought that the Peshwa would have a better chance under another Resident, he suggested his own transfer to Lucknow. The appointment of Sir Thomas Hislop to supreme control of all operations, including those in the Deccan, was felt by him to be a personal slight, though he was too loyal a servant to resent it in any way. Nevertheless, he made overtures to Sir David Ochterlony for some such post with him in Hindustán as Malcolm was holding with Hislop.

Even the visit of Malcolm was not an unmixed pleasure. On the one hand, he wrote of his friend in his diary:

'Never was anybody so frank and good-humoured. Considering his time of life [Malcolm was the senior by ten years], his activity of body and mind, his inexhaustible spirits and imperturbable temper are truly admirable; and all these qualities are accompanied with a sound judgment and a great store of knowledge derived both from reading and observation.'

But, on the other hand, Elphinstone could not conceal from himself that Malcolm's policy was at variance with his own. It was owing to Malcolm's appointment as Governor-General's Agent with Hislop that he himself was practically superseded in the affairs of the Deccan. To this, however, he had already become reconciled, through his own philosophy and the irresistible charm of Malcolm's manner. Of much more importance was the opinion that Malcolm was led to form of the Peshwa's loyalty. The soul of simplicity himself, and always inclined to over-generosity, Malcolm refused to believe in the duplicity of others, especially when their misfortunes had attracted his sympathy. He therefore allowed himself to be persuaded by the protestations of the Peshwa, that his conduct had been misinterpreted in the past, and that his honour would be redeemed by his future fidelity to the English alliance. Even long after the battle of Kirkí, Malcolm and Elphinstone agreed to differ in their estimate of Bájí Ráo's character. But in the immediate circumstances the question was one of more than academic interest. Relying upon his own interpretation of the Peshwa's motives, Malcolm encouraged him to enlist fresh troops, nominally for the protection of his frontier against the Pindárís; and at the same time he ordered the subsidiary force under General Smith to march northwards in support of Hislop's grand army. In fact, the aim of Malcolm's visit to Poona was to subordinate everything to the success of the main campaign in Central India; and the direct result was to deprive the new treaty with the Peshwa of its sole sanction, in the superiority of the British force on the spot.

Needless to say that Elphinstone did not share Malcolm's illusions as to the loyalty of the Peshwa, though he readily admitted that the supreme crisis would turn upon the attitude of the two great military chiefs, Sindia and Holkar. The chivalry of his nature shone forth conspicuously at this time, when his entire scheme of policy was being over-ruled by one who, though a friend, was also a rival, and when even his own personal safety was being endangered. To this last consideration he always professed complete indifference. When plots for his assassination had formerly been brought to his notice, he wrote in his diary:

'I have always expected this part of the game to come in its season, and must take care not to be annoyed at it, now it has come. No one could ward off such designs, if really entertained; and caring about them would probably harass one in the end. I must entirely disregard them, and not allow them to attract my attention. I should be ashamed if they even gave me an uneasy hour.'

It was a more difficult task to remove the apprehensions, on military grounds, of General Smith, who went so far as to draw up a strong remonstrance, and place it in Elphinstone's hands for transmission to

Government. Elphinstone wrote back to him that he quite agreed with his sentiments, but that he did not think the expression of them would do General Smith any good at headquarters.

'I think we risk a good deal by sending all the troops out of this country, after encouraging the Peshwa to put himself into a situation to profit by the absence of our troops, as soon as any checks encourage him to attempt it. But I would rather run a good deal of risk in that way than have your force thrown out of the campaign. ... I shall keep your letter until I hear from you again, and then either forward it or tear it as you think best.'

Malcolm's visit to Poona took place in the first fortnight of August, 1817. Within two months the fears of Elphinstone had been realised, though he did his best to postpone the crisis, 'for fear of interfering with our negotiations at Gwalior by any appearance of rupture here.' All that he could do was to watch the Peshwa, and make the best military arrangements with the few troops at his disposal. The most formidable feature was the success of the Peshwa in his plan for levying troops, suggested by Malcolm, which was accompanied by an unexpected increase of popularity. He called out the feudal levies of the Jagírdárs, who owed their very existence to Elphinstone's intervention; and thus collected at Poona about 25,000 horse and half as many foot. To oppose this army Elphinstone had immediately available only three weak battalions of Sepoys, commanded by an officer who was old and apparently not very efficient. His first precautionary measure was to order up a European regiment from Bombay; his next was to consider the removal of the cantonment from the environs of Poona to a safer distance from the city.

That Elphinstone recognised political designs behind the military assemblage is clear from the following extracts from two despatches to the Governor-General, reporting on the results of his frequent interviews with the Peshwa.

'The motive assigned in all these professions is a desire to execute the plan recommended by Sir J. Malcolm. But the troops already raised are double the number required for the service; and his Highness has taken other steps, no way connected with the defence of the country against Pindárís. Of this nature is his studied conciliation of the Rájá of Sátára, to whom he has paid attention such as has not been thought of since the power of the Peshwa was first established. He is also conciliating his brother [the Bhau] and the powerful chiefs; and he and all his principal dependents are careful to keep their property away from Poona.'

'The openness and vigour of his Highness's preparations, joined, perhaps, with some pity for his losses, and to some hope of the restoration of the Marátha greatness, render his Highness's cause more popular than it used to be; and his Highness has spared no efforts to foster these feelings and raise up odium against us. Continual reports of combinations in Hindustan, of defeats of our armies, disaffection of our troops and defections of our allies, are studiously circulated and readily believed.'

As late as the 17th of October, Elphinstone wrote in his diary:

'We shall probably have no war. At all events, I shall have no active employment, but must stay here and watch stale conspiracies.'

He hoped to the last that the personal timidity of the Peshwa would keep him quiet, until some reverse to the British arms in Central India might encourage him to action. The Peshwa's own reliance seems to have been on the success of his efforts to corrupt the Sepoys, many of whom had their families in his power.

The end was nearer than Elphinstone thought. On the 19th of October, the Hindu festival of the Dasahrá was celebrated, as usual, with a great military display, at which both the Peshwa and Elphinstone were present. Some ten thousand Marátha horse took part in it; and their circling movements round the few British troops were evidently intended to demonstrate that the latter were completely at their mercy. The intrigues with the Sepoys were carried on with increased boldness: it was ascertained that on one night 50,000 rupees and a quantity of shawls and dresses of linen were sent into the cantonment. Poona began to be deserted, for it was the universal opinion that the British were speedily to be attacked.

Elphinstone's diary, contrary to his usual practice of omitting all politics, now records the stages of the crisis:

'*October* 22*nd.* The Peshwa arming openly, and even ostentatiously. Innumerable reports and alarms of plots, conspiracies, mutinies, and assassinations. The truth seems to be that his Highness wishes to set others by the ears, and be ready himself to profit by any ill success of ours.'

'*October* 27*th*. After all kinds of warnings of plots against my life and the public peace, I have at last obtained clear and distinct information of intrigues carried on by the Peshwa with our troops, to support which he has almost surrounded our cantonment with his camps. The necessity of seeming friendly here while negotiating with Sindia prevented my resisting these dispositions. Trimbakjí is in arms again, and the whole country is in alarm. This is certainly the most embarrassing situation I have ever been placed in, and is, of course, accompanied with much anxiety; yet I never wish I were anywhere else. I look forward to the honour of defeating all these plans. I confidently hope, if I can get over this night and the two next, that I shall extricate myself and all here with credit from our perilous situation. In the meantime, I have destroyed some of my own secret papers, and am ready for the worst.'

Elphinstone's anxiety and coolness are thus described by Captain Grant (afterwards Grant Duff, the historian of the Maráthás), who was then on his staff:

'For several nights the Peshwa and his advisers had deliberated on the advantage of surprising the troops before the arrival of the European regiment; and for this purpose on October 28th their guns were yoked, their horses saddled, and their infantry in readiness. This intelligence was brought to Mr. Elphinstone a little before midnight; and for a moment it became a question whether self-defence did not require that the attack should be anticipated. The British cantonment and the Residency were perfectly still, but in the Peshwa's camp, south of the town, all was noise and uproar. As Mr. Elphinstone now stood listening on the terrace, he probably thought that in thus exposing the

THE THIRD MARÁTHÁ WAR

troops to be cut off, without even the satisfaction of dying with their arms in their hands, he had followed the system of confidence to a culpable extremity; but other motives influenced his conduct at this important moment. He was aware how little faith the other Marátha princes placed in Bájí Ráo, and that Sindia, who knew him well, would hesitate to engage in hostilities until the Peshwa had fairly committed himself. Apprised of the Governor-General's secret plans and his intended movements on Gwalior, which many circumstances might have concurred to postpone, Mr. Elphinstone had studiously avoided every appearance which might affect the negotiations in Hindustán, or by any preparation and apparent alarm on his part give Sindia's secret emissaries at Poona reason to believe that war was inevitable. To have sent to the cantonment at that hour would have occasioned considerable stir; and in the meantime, by the report of the spies, the Peshwa was evidently deliberating. The din in the city was dying away, the night was passing, and the motive which had hitherto prevented preparation determined Mr. Elphinstone to defer it some hours longer.'

Bájí Ráo threw away his last chance on the night of the 28th of October. The next morning Elphinstone wrote to the officer commanding the European regiment to come on as fast as possible, without regard to anything but the health of his men: and also requested Colonel Burr, who commanded at Poona, to keep his troops on the alert. The European regiment marched in on the afternoon of the 30th of October. Elphinstone now felt justified in carrying into execution a decisive step which he had been contemplating for some time—the removal of the troops from an ill-chosen position near the city to Kirkí, some four miles northwards, where they would be secure against a surprise, and free from the solicitations of the Peshwa's emissaries. At about the same time, General Smith, acting on his own view of the situation, concentrated his own troops, who were scattered along the frontier, and sent back one battalion towards Poona.

Elphinstone himself continued at the Residency, with a slight guard of Sepoys. From here he could behold the increasing aggressiveness of the Maráthás. They plundered the old cantonment, rode exultingly under the walls of the Residency, and began to form a camp half-way towards the new British position. An English officer was attacked, wounded, and robbed of his horse, two miles out of the city, on the Bombay road. The report was everywhere spread that the Firinghís had fled before the invincible arms of Srimant, and would soon be driven out of the country.

On the morning of the 5th of November, the Peshwa sent a trusted servant to say that he was determined to bring things to an early settlement: Let the European regiment, therefore, be sent away, and the native brigade reduced to its usual strength; let the cantonment also be removed to a place to be pointed out by himself. On these terms he would continue his friendship with the British Government. Otherwise, he would mount his horse and leave Poona, never to return until his terms had been accepted. To this blustering message Elphinstone replied that he was still anxious for peace, and would not cross the river that separated Kirkí from Poona; but that if the Peshwa's troops advanced, he should be obliged to attack them.

Within an hour after the departure of the envoy, large bodies of Maráthás began to stream out in the direction of the new cantonment, in such a manner as to cut off the direct road thither from the Residency. The rest of the story may be told in Elphinstone's words:

'We had only time to leave the Residency with the clothes on our backs, and crossing the river at a ford, march off to the Kirki bridge with the river between us and the enemy, and a little firing but no real fighting. The Residency, with all the records, and all my books, journals, letters, manuscripts, &c., was soon in a blaze. While the men and followers were fording, we went ourselves to observe the enemy. The sight was magnificent as the tide rolled out of Poona. Grant . . . described it as resembling the bore in the Gulf of Cambay. Everything was hushed except the trampling and neighing of horses, and the whole valley was filled with them like a river in flood. I had always told Colonel Burr that, when war broke out, we must recover our character by a forward movement that should encourage and fix our own men, while it checked our enemies; and I now . . . sent an order to move down at once and attack. . . . When opposite to a *nala* [water-course] we halted (injudiciously, I think) to cannonade, and at the same moment the enemy began from twelve or fifteen guns. Soon after, his whole mass of cavalry came on at speed in the most splendid style. The rush of horse, the sound of the earth, the waving of flags, the brandishing of spears, were grand beyond description, but perfectly ineffectual. One great body, however, formed on our left and rear; and when one of our native battalions was drawn off by its ardour to attack Major Pinto [a Portuguese in the Peshwa's service], this body charged with great vigour and broke through between it and the European regiment. At this time, the rest of the line were pretty well occupied with shot, matchlocks, and above all with rockets; and I own I thought there was a good chance of our losing the battle. The native battalion, however, though it had expended all its ammunition, survived the charge, and was brought back to the line by Colonel Burr, who showed infinite coolness and courage. And after some more firing, and some advancing, together with detaching a few companies towards a hill on our right, we found ourselves alone on the field, and the sun long set. I was at first for advancing to the water at the Séth's Garden, but was persuaded it was better to return to camp, which it was.'

Such was the battle of Kirkí, as told without any exaggeration of the part played in it by the narrator. It is impossible not to be struck by the tactical insight, the boldness, and the coolness of judgment, worthy of one who had served his first campaign under Wellington. Elphinstone's services as diplomatist and soldier were thus recognised by Canning in the House of Commons, when moving a vote of thanks to Lord Hastings and his army, after the termination of the war:

'While the campaign was proceeding thus successfully against those whom Lord Hastings had taken into account as probable enemies, their number was unexpectedly increased by the addition of the Peshwa, the executive head of the Marátha empire, who suddenly broke the ties which bound him in strictest amity to the British Government. Even Sir John Malcolm—better qualified perhaps than any other person to fathom the designs and estimate the sincerity of the native powers—had been so far imposed upon, in an interview with that prince at Poona, as to express to Lord Hastings his perfect conviction that the friendly professions of the Peshwa deserved entire confidence. In the midst of this unsuspecting tranquillity—at a moment now known to have been concerted with the other Marátha chieftains—the Peshwa manifested his real intention by an unprovoked attack upon the Residency at Poona. Mr. Elphinstone (a name distinguished in the literature as well as in the politics of the East) exhibited, on that trying occasion, military courage and skill which, though valuable accessories to diplomatic talents, we are not entitled to require as necessary qualifications for civil employment. On that, and not on that occasion only, but on many others in the course of this singular campaign, Mr. Elphinstone displayed talents and resources, which would have rendered him no mean general in a country where generals are of no mean excellence and reputation.'

In military history, the battle of Kirkí does not hold a very conspicuous place. The British force consisted of less than 3000 men; of whom about 20 were killed and about 70 wounded. The army of the Peshwa is said to have numbered 18.000 cavalry and 8000 infantry; and their loss is estimated at several hundreds, including a general with the odd name of Moro Dixit. . But the political result was far more decisive than these figures might imply. The British ascendency in arms, which had seriously suffered in the minds of the people, was at once re-established. A few days afterwards, when General Smith arrived with the subsidiary force, the Peshwa fled from his

capital, which he was destined never again to behold.
The war henceforth resolved itself into a prolonged
chase after the Peshwa, varied with occasional engagements and sieges of the hill-fortresses, which had been
the historic strongholds of the Maráthás from the days
of Sivají. General Pritzler was detached from the
grand army to co-operate with General Smith; and
both were placed under the orders of Elphinstone,
who had no little difficulty in reconciling their rival
pretensions. The southern portions of the Peshwa's
dominions were meanwhile occupied by a force from
Madras, under Munro, whose masterly achievements
were thus commemorated by Canning in the speech
above referred to :—

'At the southern extremity of this long line of operations,
and in a part of the campaign carried on in a district far
from public gaze, was employed a man whose name I should
indeed have been sorry to have passed over in silence.
I allude to Colonel Thomas Munro, a gentleman of whose
rare qualifications the late House of Commons had opportunities of judging at their bar, on the renewal of the East
India Company's charter; and than whom Europe never
produced a more accomplished statesman, nor India, so
fertile in heroes, a more skilful soldier. This gentleman,
whose occupations for some years must have been rather of a
civil and administrative than a military nature, was called
early in the war to exercise abilities which, though dormant,
had not rusted from disuse. He went into the field with
not more than five or six hundred men, of whom a very
small proportion were Europeans, and marched into the
Marátha territories to take possession of the country which
had been ceded to us by the treaty of Poona. The popula-

tion which he subjugated by arms, he managed with such address, equity, and wisdom, that he established an empire over their hearts and feelings. Nine forts were surrendered to him or taken by assault on his way; and at the end of a silent and scarcely observed progress, he emerged from a territory heretofore hostile to the British interest, with an accession instead of a diminution of force, leaving everything secure and tranquil behind him.'

The conquest of the Deccan occupied altogether some five months, while the Peshwa, who ultimately fled to Berár and then to Central India, did not surrender to Malcolm until June, 1818. It is unnecessary to follow the course of this tedious campaign; but one or two incidents are, perhaps, sufficiently interesting to be recorded here. After the flight of the Peshwa from Poona, Elphinstone's first care was to protect the city from his own Sepoys, who vowed vengeance for the outrages that had been inflicted upon their own stragglers and relations. This was managed by the excellent arrangements of General Smith (to whom Elphinstone gives all the credit), assisted by a deputation of native bankers. The advantages that resulted were—not only 'to maintain our general reputation, and to conciliate friends in the present contest, but also to preserve a very fertile source of supply of money and of commodities for the army.'

In the second month of the war, when the Peshwa's army was still unsubdued, and when its precise position was unknown, was fought the battle of Koregáon, which is still remembered with pride by the Bombay

Army. A weak battalion of Sepoys, less than 500 strong, had been injudiciously summoned from Sirur to reinforce the garrison at Poona. After marching all one night it found itself in the morning on the river Bhima, face to face with the whole army of the Peshwa. Bájí Ráo himself, with his Sardárs, sat on a hill two miles off, to witness the battle. Cut off from their only water-supply in the river, the little force entrenched itself in the village of Koregáon, where through the whole of the day and part of the following night it resisted the attacks of the enemy. The Marátha horse repeatedly charged into the village, which was also scorched by showers of rockets; but the most formidable opponents were found in the Arab sharpshooters, of whom we hear much during this war. Besides terrible sufferings from thirst, hunger, and fatigue, the Sepoys lost more than half their number in killed and wounded, including six British officers out of eight. At last, when the situation seemed desperate, the enemy's fire began to slacken, and they were presently in full retreat, alarmed by the news of General Smith's approach. Elphinstone accompanied the general to the scene two days afterwards, and his comments are not without psychological interest: 'Our men could not be got to storm. The Europeans talked of surrendering. The native officers behaved very ill; and the men latterly could scarce be got, even by kicks and blows, to form small parties to defend themselves, . . . Most that I have seen tried to excuse themselves, and are surprised to find that they are thought to have done a great action: yet an action really greater has seldom been achieved—a strong incitement never to despair.'

On the same day (January 5, 1818) that Elphinstone describes the battle of Koregáon, he mysteriously enters in his diary, 'many letters, one announcing great change to me and to all.' There was need for secrecy. All his correspondence at this time was written on the smallest slips of paper, to be rolled up and conveyed in quills. This particular letter brought the result of the deliberations of Lord Hastings with regard to the future of the Deccan. The Peshwa was announced to have forfeited his throne; a small principality was to be set apart for the Rájá of Sátára; but the rest of Bájí Ráo's wide dominions were declared British territory, under the administration of Elphinstone as Commissioner. But these instructions were not made public for some little while longer. The hill-forts in the Gháts still held out; while the Rájá of Sátára, whose person had been seized by the Peshwa at an early stage in the war, was now being dragged in his company backwards and forwards through the Deccan.

Early in February, the *petta* (town) and fortress of Sátára were occupied without serious resistance. After the British flag had been hoisted on the fort for a moment, it was pulled down and replaced by the flag of the Rájá, as a sign of his sovereignty. Ten days later General Smith managed to bring to bay the main body of the Peshwa's army at Ashtí, about a hundred miles due east from Poona. Gokla, the only Maráthá general who had shown much energy, was killed in a cavalry charge; the Peshwa himself escaped for the time to Nágpur territory; but the Rájá of Sátára and his family fell into the hands of the victors.

Elphinstone now felt himself justified in issuing a long proclamation, in Maráthí, addressed to the people of the Deccan, reciting the story of the perfidy and violence of the Peshwa, which had compelled the British to drive him from his throne and conquer his dominions, and stating that a portion of his territory would be reserved for the Rájá of Sátára.

'The rest of the country will be held by the Honourable Company. The revenues will be collected for the Government, but all property, real or personal, will be secured. All *wattan* and *inám* [grants of land revenue-free], annual stipends, and all religious and charitable establishments will be protected, and all religious sects will be tolerated, and their customs maintained, as far as is just and reasonable. The farming system is abolished. Officers will be forthwith appointed, to collect a regular and moderate revenue on the part of the British Government, to administer justice and to encourage the cultivation of the soil. They will be authorised to allow of remissions, in consideration of the circumstances of the times.'

It remains to chronicle briefly the other incidents of the war. Sindia remained quiet, overawed by the grand army, or won over through the diplomacy of Malcolm. At Nágpur, the same drama was enacted as at Poona, a few weeks later. The Resident, Jenkins, was suddenly attacked on the hill of Sítabáldí

THE THIRD MARÁTHÁ WAR 119

by all the forces of the Rájá. The garrison, consisting of less than 1400 Sepoys, were at first thrown into confusion, but were finally saved by an heroic charge of three troops of Madras native cavalry. The Rájá fled, but a successor to the throne was found in an infant of his family. In Central India the campaign was short but sharp. Holkar himself was only a boy, but his generals resolved to try the hazard of the die. They were decisively defeated at the battle of Mehidpur, in which Malcolm figured conspicuously. By the treaty that followed, Holkar lost his outlying provinces and his claims over the Rájput princes, but still remained the foremost power in Málwá. The Pindárís, the original cause of the war, gave comparatively little trouble. The greatest of their chiefs, Amír Khán, prudently accepted the liberal terms offered him, in accordance with which his successor is now in possession of the principality of Tonk. The military array of the others was easily broken up; their leaders took refuge in the jungle, where one of them is said to have been eaten by a tiger. The final pacification of Central India afforded congenial employment to Malcolm for the next twelve months.

Nearly forty years later, in the time of Dalhousie. the States of Nágpur and Sátára fell to the Paramount Power, by the application of the doctrine of lapse. But with that exception, the settlement effected after the Third Marátha War has continued unimpaired to the present day. Putting aside the Southern Marátha States, three great Marátha princes—Sindia, Holkar, and the Gáckwár—still rule over territory aggregating 46,000 square miles, with more than seven million inhabitants, and an estimated revenue of three millions sterling. But not a fragment of their widely scattered dominions lies within the country that uses Maráthí for its vernacular.

CHAPTER IX

THE SETTLEMENT OF THE DECCAN

1818—1819

ELPHINSTONE received his appointment as Commissioner for the settlement of the Deccan in January, 1818; but several months had to pass before civil authority was everywhere restored. During March and April he accompanied the force detached for the capture of the hill-fortresses in the Ghâts, some of which held out until bombarded. A pleasant interlude was the formal restoration of the Râjâ of Sâtâra to the throne of Sivají. Lord Hastings had left Elphinstone the choice of giving the Râjâ a sovereignty, or only a *jagír*. He adopted the former alternative, because he recognised the importance ' of leaving for part of the Peshwa's subjects a government which could afford them service in their own way.' The British District of Sâtâra, which represents the State then constituted, has an area of 5000 square miles and a population of one million souls.

Elphinstone was much attracted to the young prince, who did not fail to requite the good-will shown to him.

'*March* 4. . . . Visited the Rájá. He kept up the forms of sovereignty, neither rising nor bowing; but in his language and manners was civil and compliant. He is about twenty; not handsome, but good-humoured and frank. His brothers have nearly the same character, with rather better looks. His mother is a fine old lady, who has been handsome, and has still very fine eyes. She has good manners, and, it is said, good abilities. The Rájá's gratitude to General Smith, which seemed as unfeigned as his joy at his deliverance, was very engaging.'

'*April* 22 [after the installation]. The Rájá gave me an entertainment in the evening; and after advice and good wishes I took leave, much interested in the brothers, whose concord, simplicity, and attachment to their mother and each other are very amiable.'

It is gratifying to know that Elphinstone's favourable anticipations were realised. Writing to Strachey, nearly five years later (December, 1822), he says:—

'I must tell you what a good fellow the little Rájá of Sátára is. When I visited him, we sat on two *masnads* [cushions] without exchanging one single word, in a very respectable *darbár*; but the moment we retired to a *khilwat* [cabinet] the Rájá produced his civil and criminal register, and his minute of [revenue] demands, collections, and balances for the last quarter, and began explaining the state of his country as eagerly as a young Collector. He always sits in the Nyáyádish (court of justice) and conducts his business with the utmost regularity. I hunted with him the day we parted; and a young gentleman had a bad fall just in front of me, and lay for dead. When I got off, I found a horseman dismounted and supporting his head; and, to my surprise, it was the Rájá, who had let his horse go and run to his assistance. The Rájá's turning out well is principally owing to Captain Grant, the Resident, formerly adjutant to the grenadier battalion, and now historian of the Marátha empire.'

And again, in November, 1826:—

'The Rájá of Sátára is the most civilised Marátha I ever met with, has his country in excellent order, and everything, to his roads and acqueducts, in a style that would do credit to a European. I was more struck with his private sitting-room than anything I saw at Sátára. It contains a single table covered with green velvet, at which the descendant of Sivají sits in a chair, and writes letters, as well as a journal of his transactions, with his own hand.... He gave me at parting the identical *bághnakh* (literally, tiger's claws) with which Sivají seized the Mughal general in a treacherous embrace when he stabbed him and afterwards destroyed his army. They are most formidable steel hooks, very sharp, and attached to two rings fitting the fingers, and lie concealed in the inside of the hand [1].'

Elphinstone could thus make as well as unmake a king, and he took more delight in the former task than in the latter. He was now to show that he possessed the talents of an administrator, in addition to those of a diplomatist and a general. Since his early days at Benares, he had had no experience of civil work; but he had then imbibed from Mr. Davis an unfavourable opinion of the Bengal system, which was confirmed by the publication about this time of the Report of the Parliamentary Committee of 1812. He was fond of telling a story to illustrate the

[1] This weapon is now in the possession of Sir M. E. Grant Duff, Elphinstone's godson.

dread which our courts of law and our Regulations inspired among the natives. When the North-West was first annexed, the inhabitants of a newly occupied village were encountered in full flight. Asked if Lord Lake was coming, 'No,' they replied, 'the Adálat is coming,' the Adálat being the name of the British tribunal now represented by the Civil Court. With these views it will readily be believed that Elphinstone thought it his first duty to preserve as much as possible of the existing system of administration, not, of course, as being the ideally best, but as the best under all the circumstances and for the time. He knew that the Adálat and the Regulations would ultimately have to be introduced; but he was desirous of postponing their introduction, and of developing in the meantime all that could be discovered of good in the native institutions. In acknowledging the receipt from his friend Erskine of a treatise of Bentham's (which he afterwards studied diligently), he added;—

'I have not, however, so much occasion as you suppose for instruction in the principles of legislation; for my employment is very humble. It is to learn which system is in force, and to preserve it unimpaired. This, I think, ought to be the great duty of a provisional government; and I shall think I have done a great service to this country if I can prevent people making laws for it until they see whether it wants them.'

The result of Elphinstone's enquiries is contained in his 'Report on the Territories conquered from the Peshwa,' which was not submitted to the Supreme

Government until the close of 1819, when he had already left Poona for Bombay. The Report[1] begins with a descriptive account of the country and a sketch of Maráthá history, and then reviews elaborately the Marátha system of administration, in the several departments of revenue, and civil and criminal jurisdiction. Its interest now is, of course, mainly historical, as a record of a state of things that has passed away; but, like everything Elphinstone wrote, it is replete with philosophic reflections, which will always retain their value. It also contains the principles that guided his own reforms, many of which were carried out subsequently, during the period when he was Governor of Bombay. It will be convenient, therefore, to disregard strict chronological order, and to treat the settlement of the Deccan under its several headings— political, fiscal, and judicial.

Elphinstone estimates the total area of the country placed under his administration at 50,000 square miles, and guesses the inhabitants at four millions, or only eighty persons per square mile[2]. He is careful to distinguish three tracts, differing both in physical aspects and in population. In the extreme north is the hot and low-lying plain of Khándesh, occupying the valley of the Tápti between two mountain ranges.

[1] First printed in full in Mr. Forrest's volume of *Selections*, though before well known as an official document and from extracts.
[2] According to the Census of 1881, the nine British districts into which the Deccan is now divided had an area of 52,356 square miles and a population of 7,700,537 souls, being an average of 147 per square mile.

This tract had not recovered from the calamitous famine of 1803. It was placed in charge of Captain Briggs, who devoted himself to repressing the ravages of the wild tribe of Bhíls, and to inviting immigrants to cultivate the waste but fertile fields. Next comes the Marátha country proper, comprising the districts of Ahmadnagar and Poona, and the newly formed State of Sátára. Westward it is bounded by the main range of the Gháts, southward by the Kistna river, while eastward it stretches toward the plateau of the Deccan. Here was the home of the Marátha nation; here they built their mountain fortresses, fondly deemed impregnable; here they bred and pastured their hardy ponies. Of the Bráhmans and soldiers Elphinstone expresses a very unfavourable opinion. The character he gives of the peasantry will be recognised as true in its main features at the present day:—

'The Marátha peasantry have some pride in the triumphs of their nation, and some ambition to partake in its military exploits; but although circumstances might turn them into soldiers or robbers, at present their habits are decidedly peaceful. They are sober, frugal, industrious; mild and inoffensive to everybody; and among themselves neither dishonest nor insincere. The faults of their government have, however, created the corresponding vices in them: its oppression and extortion have taught them dissimulation, mendacity, and fraud; and the insecurity of property has rendered them so careless of the future, as to lavish on a marriage or other ceremony the savings of years of parsimony. . . . The effects of this last are felt in the debts and embarrassments in which the whole of the agricultural population is plunged.'

The last of the three tracts is the Maráthá Karnatik, extending from the Kistna southwards to the frontiers of Mysore and the ceded districts of the Madras Presidency. In addition to the districts of Belgáum and Bijápur, it includes the Southern Marátha Jagírs. It is extremely fertile, comprising wide plains of the famous black cotton soil. The inhabitants speak Kanarese, and always hated the Maráthás as foreign invaders. They had readily joined General Munro in expelling their rulers, and are described as perfectly quiet and well affected. The administrator was Mr. Chaplin, an experienced member of the Madras Civil Service.

Elphinstone had hoped to enjoy the co-operation of Munro in effecting the settlement of the Karnatik, which Munro had already conquered by arms. He had to be content with a searching correspondence, and a brief visit of five days. After Munro's departure he wrote in his diary:—

'I have gained a great deal of instruction from him, and have been greatly pleased with his strong practical good sense, his simplicity and frankness, his perfect good-nature and good-humour, his real benevolence, unmixed with the slightest cant of misanthropy, his activity and his truthfulness of mind, easily pleased with anything, and delighted with those things that in general have no effect but on a youthful imagination. The effect of these last qualities is heightened by their contrast with his stern countenance and searching eye.'

Munro, though not yet Governor of Madras, had spent all his life in organising the administrative system in the ceded and conquered districts of that Presidency. It was from his example that Elphinstone learned the duty of investigating thoroughly the indigenous institutions, and the supreme importance of introducing the least possible change. With Malcolm he shared (though from more philosophical motives) the policy of sympathy, and a generous recognition of native prejudices and native aspirations. At about this time he wrote in his diary:—

'Malcolm certainly has wise and enlarged views of policy; and, among them, the kind and indulgent manner in which he regards the natives (though perhaps originating in his heart as much as in his head) is by no means the least important. It appears to particular advantage in his feelings towards the native army, and in the doctrines he has inculcated regarding them. It is melancholy to think that he is not young, and that he is the last of the class of politicians to which he belongs. The later statesmen are certainly more imperious and harsher in their notions, and are inferior in wisdom, inasmuch as they reckon more on force than he does, and less on affection.'

With Malcolm and Munro for his guides, Elphinstone proceeded apace with his dual task of conciliation and inquiry. When the Peshwa had been chased out of his dominions, and the hill-forts had fallen one by one, all organised opposition ceased. The restoration of the Rájá of Sátára, and the maintenance of the Southern Jagírdárs, showed that the British had no intention of disregarding Maráthá sentiments. As always happens in India after a conquest, the cultivators, who form the vast mass of the population, acquiesced in the change of their rulers with hardly a murmur. But Elphinstone was far too prudent to interpret this acquiescence as meaning active contentment; and he was also well aware of the influence exercised by the classes who had necessarily suffered from the revolution. The disbanded soldiers of the Peshwa were to some extent provided for in the irregular levies of the Company (*sibandis*), that were raised to keep order; every consideration was shown for those who, either as officials or landowners, had ranked as gentlemen under Marátha rule: while the numerous caste of Poona Bráhmans, who had lost most of all by the overthrow of a Bráhman government, were studiously conciliated by a series of measures adopted for their express benefit.

'The general disposition of the agricultural class,' Elphinstone wrote in an official dispatch, not reprinted by Forrest, 'is strong in favour of tranquillity. They are the first sufferers by wars or by assemblages of banditti; and as they were by no means favoured under the Bráhman government, they cannot, whatever pride they may take in Marátha independence, seriously wait [? wish] for its restoration. But,' he adds, 'even among them there are many drawbacks on the gratitude we might expect from our light assessment and protection. The *desmukhs* and other *zamindárs*, the *patéls* and other village authorities, who lose power by our care to prevent exactions, have probably influence sufficient to injure us with the very people for whose cause we incur their odium. The whole of the soldiery and all connected with them—all who lived entirely by service, all who joined service and cultivation, all who had a brother in employment who is now thrown back on the family, and all who had horses and were otherwise maintained by the existence of an army—detest us and our regular battalions, and are joined by their neighbours from sympathy and national feeling.'

The Jagírdárs belonged to two classes: the great hereditary nobles, whose political status had already been recognised, and fixed by the settlement of Pandarpur [1]; and those of inferior rank, who had hitherto held their estates at pleasure. With regard to the former class, not much difficulty was experienced. It was only necessary that they should transfer their allegiance from the Peshwa to the Company. To this they all consented, with a single exception. Chintáman Ráo, one of the Patwardhans, a Bráhman family who had received large grants from the Peshwa, refused, on the grotesque plea that it was nowhere stipulated in the settlement of Pandarpur that, 'in the event of disagreement between the Peshwa and the British Government, I am to serve the latter.' The threat of resumption and the personal intervention of Elphinstone were required to remove these and other scruples. Chintáman Ráo is described as having 'a narrow and crooked understanding, a litigious spirit, and a capricious temper.' 'Our intercourse,' however, 'completely restored his good humour, and had latterly the appearance of complete cordiality and satisfaction, which, though it may not be lasting, I have no doubt is perfectly sincere.'

[1] See *ante*, pp. 77-79.

The terms granted to these greater Jagírdárs were liberal. They received assurances that their rank and dignity would be maintained as in the time of the Peshwa; and that the British Government would not interfere, except in case of very flagrant abuse of power, or long continuance of gross mismanagement. In particular, their local jurisdiction, including the power of life and death, was guaranteed to them; and in compliance with their earnest entreaties, they were granted a special exemption from the Adálats (Civil Courts) of the Presidency. Though their claims to the right of private war could not be sanctioned, it was arranged that any matters of difference among themselves should be regarded as 'political,' to be dealt with by direct orders from the Government, and not under the Regulations applicable to British territory. Another fertile source of dispute was anticipated by provisions for the extradition of criminals, and for pursuing them into the dominions of the chiefs.

The case of the inferior Jagírdárs presented more complications, and also more difficulty. Elphinstone's constant desire was to preserve them as an upper class of society, intermediate between the cultivators and the officials, though he was well aware of the impossibility of effecting this by artificial means. He saw them disappearing before his eyes, but he did everything in his power to delay the inevitable result. He often thought over the desirability of rewarding native officials with grants of land instead of pensions.

A few years later, when at Bombay, he thus explained his general policy, in a despatch to the Supreme Government, which seems to have been called forth by some threat of resumptions:

'The maintenance of many of the chiefs in their possessions was certainly suggested, as supposed by the Governor-General, for the purpose of avoiding popular discontent, and preventing the too rapid fall of great families; but in other cases it rested on the belief that the holders were entitled of right to their possessions. Where a *jagír* was by the original grant made hereditary in the family of the grantee, there could be no doubt of the right of the descendant; but where there was no such grant (as was the case with almost all the *jagírs*), the right rested on different grounds. . . . A *jagír* was usually granted during life, for the purpose of maintaining troops to serve the State; a small portion was set aside as a personal provision for the chief. This mode of maintaining troops being always kept up, there was no motive for removing the *jagírdár*, and consequently every grant was renewed on the death of each incumbent, his son paying a relief to the government. When this practice had long subsisted, the *jagír* came to be regarded as hereditary, and the resumption of it would have been viewed as a violation of private property. The nature and history of *jagírs* has so great an analogy to those of feudal benefices, that the manner in which this transition took place can be easily understood in Europe. The period for which a *jagír* had been held was, therefore, a very important point to advert to in deciding how long to continue it. I recommended that all granted by the Mughal Emperors or the Rájás of Sátára should be hereditary in the fullest sense of the word. . . . The *jagírdárs* of the Peshwas stood on a different footing. They had arisen under the dynasty we had subverted: none could have been in possession for more than seventy years; and they had been kept in mind by the exaction of service, as well as by occasional resumptions, of the real nature and extent of their tenure. Much consideration was, however, due to them as the actual possessors of power; and they were allowed to retain their personal lands for one or more generations, according to their merits or importance.'

Besides this lenicncy in the matter of resumption. Elphinstone also granted to the lesser Jagírdárs a recognition of their privileged status which was particularly welcome to them. They were all alike exempted from the ordinary process of the Adálat (Civil Court). In criminal matters they were made subject to the jurisdiction of the Collector in his capacity of political agent, though not without previous reference to the Commissioner. Elphinstone, indeed, proposed to extend the same indulgence to all persons of rank, at least during the lives of the existing generation. This policy afterwards received the warm support of Malcolm, who reported ten years later that—

'There is nothing in the new code that creates inconvenience or embarrassment from the existence or extension of the privileged classes of the Deccan. I can confidently state that, during my whole experience in India, I have known no institution so prized by those who enjoy its exemptions, or more gratifying to the whole people among whom it was established. It is recognised by the lowest orders as a concession in forms to those whom they deem their superiors, and as such is received as a boon by the community who, from their condition, neither understand nor appreciate those unyielding forms that deny alike advantages of birth and the claims of rank and service.'

The Bráhmans showed themselves less amenable to conciliation, almost justifying the character Captain Grant gave them as 'generally discontented, and only restrained by fear from being treasonable.' The best that Elphinstone himself could find to say of them is: 'There are among them many instances of decent and respectable lives; and although they are generally subtle and insincere, I have met with some on whom I could depend for sound and candid opinions.' How much they had lost by the downfall of the Peshwa may be gathered from a few facts recorded in another connexion. Bájí Ráo, though he reduced the former expenditure, still used to give a small sum to each of 50,000 Bráhmans. Both he and also his Sardárs and Ministers employed many learned Bráhmans in various offices connected with the Hindu ritual; while all, on religious principle, allowed stipends and grants of land to many others for whose services they had no occasion. Under the name of the Dakshina, the sum of five *lakhs* of rupees (£50,000) was annually distributed by the Peshwa among Bráhmans, nominally as a reward for learning, but in practice as a mere almsgiving. In fact, Elphinstone goes so far as to say that 'one of the principal objects of the Peshwa's government was the maintenance of the Bráhmans.'

Needless to say that Elphinstone, though no student of Sanskrit, was absolutely free from any prejudice against the legendary superstitions of the

Hindu religion. He was, indeed, tolerant enough to propose the endowment (out of the Dakshina) of professorships for the teaching of Hindu divinity and mythology. His sympathy also was aroused by the stories he had heard of great numbers of Bráhmans reduced to such distress as to be subsisting on the sale of shawls and other presents which they had received in better times. What he could do for this impoverished class he did willingly. The Sátára proclamation contained a clause expressly guaranteeing to them quiet possession of their grants of land and pecuniary allowances. After order was restored, one of his first acts was to ratify this assurance publicly at Násik, a very holy place of pilgrimage; and to accompany his words with a distribution of alms, which was afterwards repeated at Poona. Out of the Dakshina, he originally proposed to set apart £20,000 for religious expenses, including two colleges for Bráhmans. But considerations of economy compelled him to restrict this design to a grant of £5000 a year for prizes in Sanskrit learning, which forms the nucleus of the existing Poona College.

Despite these generous provisions, it was from the Bráhmans of Poona that Elphinstone experienced the only serious attempt to shake off British rule. A conspiracy was formed to murder all the Europeans, to seize the hill-forts, and to take possession of the person of the Rájá of Sátára. The plot was detected, and those who had taken part in it were promptly and severely dealt with. Elphinstone ordered the ringleaders to be executed by being blown from guns [1], remarking that this mode of execution 'contains two valuable elements of capital punishment: it is painless to the criminal and terrible to the beholder.' When Sir Evan Nepean (Governor of Bombay) suggested to Elphinstone that it would be prudent to apply to the Supreme Government for an indemnity, he replied, with true Roman dignity: 'If I have done wrong, I deserve to be punished; if I have done right, I do not require an indemnity.'

Elphinstone's fiscal reforms may be treated very shortly. In this, even more than in other matters, he was content mainly to record and preserve the system that he found in existence; while it would be hopeless to attempt to interest English readers in the *jamabandi* (revenue-assessment) of a Marátha province seventy years ago. Suffice it to say that he abolished the farming system, which had but recently been introduced as a refined engine of extortion; and that his general instructions to the Collectors were:

'maintain the native system; levy the revenue according to the actual cultivation; make the assessments light; impose no new taxes, and do away with none unless obviously unjust; above all, make no innovations.'

Every exertion seems to have been honestly made to relieve the cultivators from excessive exactions.

[1] Sir T. E. Colebrooke describes this as a Marátha punishment, and as an innovation in British India. We have read somewhere that it is of Mughal introduction; it was certainly used by Sir Hector Munro, in 1764, to decimate his mutinous sepoys shortly before the battle of Baksár.

'The foundation for the assessment in all cases was the amount paid by each village in times when the people considered themselves to have been well governed. Deductions were made from this in proportion to the diminution of the cultivation, and afterwards further allowances were made on any specific grounds alleged by the *ráyats* (cultivators). The amount to be paid was partitioned among the *ráyats* by the village officers; and if all were satisfied *patas* (leases) were given, and the settlement was ended. ... All the Collectors kept up the principle of the *ráyatwári* settlement[1], and some carried it to a greater extent than had been usual with the Maráthás.'

Notwithstanding all these efforts at moderation, there can be little doubt that the early assessment of the Deccan, as of other provinces when they first came under British administration, was higher than the people could afford to pay. The causes of this appear to have been—(1) the adoption of native rent-rolls, which represented not actual payments, but the highest standard ever attained; and (2) the uniform exaction of the demand by British officials, without sufficient regard to the character of the seasons or other varying circumstances. And it must always be borne in mind that in those days a superabundant harvest was regarded as a calamity only second to a general failure; for when there was little local traffic, and no exportation, low prices meant reduced profits to the cultivators.

[1] The system of fixing the amount due from each cultivator, which had already been introduced in Madras by Munro, as opposed to the *zamíndári* or landlord system of Bengal.

The land-revenue was, of course, the sheet-anchor of finance. But there were also several subordinate sources of income—such as *zakát*, or customs; *abkárí*, or excise; *nazars*, or fines paid on succession to property, chiefly in cases of adoption; fees paid by wandering shepherds for the right to pasture their flocks on waste lands; and fees paid for leave to cut wood in government forests. Of these, customs produced about £50,000 a year. This was a transit duty levied by the bullock-load; but the rate varied in proportion to the value of the commodity, the highest being eight rupees (16s.). It was levied independently in each district, so that goods were liable to be repeatedly stopped and searched. To remedy this inconvenience, there was a class who undertook for a single payment to pass goods through the whole country. Elphinstone continued the farming of customs as a temporary measure. The only reform he introduced was to abolish the privilege of exemption which had been enjoyed by our camp-dealers, in order to prevent disputes with the Peshwa's officials. Excise, which even at this time was an important source of revenue in Bengal, did not yield over £1000 a year. The use of spirituous liquors was forbidden at Poona, and discouraged everywhere else. Drunkenness was almost unknown in the Marátha country, 'which had thus a decided superiority in morals over the old provinces.' Elphinstone recommended a policy of prohibition, or at any rate a very high rate of taxation. He also approved the tax on adoptions, as being one that was little felt, and as attended with advantages in recording successions. Of a special duty on salt we hear nothing. So far as it was taxed at all, it was included under customs.

Police and criminal justice occupy together more than thirty pages in Elphinstone's Report, which form very interesting reading, partly because of their historical information, and partly because of Elphinstone's enlightened criticisms. On the whole, he was favourably impressed with the indigenous system of village watch and ward, though he recognised the difficulty of preserving its useful features under British administration. The essence of the system was the union of fiscal and executive authority in the same hands. The *patel* (head-man) was responsible both for the land-revenue and for the police of his village. If occasion required it, he might call upon all the inhabitants for assistance; but his immediate deputy in matters of police was the village watchman, named *mhár* among the Maráthás, and always a Dher by caste.

'His duties are to keep watch at night, to find out all arrivals and departures, observe all strangers, and report all suspicious persons to the *patél*. He is likewise bound to know the character of every man in the village; and, in the event of a theft committed within the village bounds, it is his business to detect the thief. He is enabled to do this by his early habits of inquisitiveness and observation, as well as by the nature of his allowance, which being partly a small share of the grain and similar property belonging to each house, he is kept always on the watch to ascertain his fees, and always in motion to collect them. When a theft or robbery happens, the watchman commences his inquiries and researches. It is very common for him to track a thief by his footsteps; and if he does this to another village, so as to satisfy the watchman there, or if he otherwise traces the property to an adjoining village, his responsibility ends, and it is the duty of the watchman of the new village to take up the pursuit. The last village to which the thief has been clearly traced becomes answerable for the property stolen, which would otherwise fall on the village where the robbery was committed. The watchman is obliged to make up this amount as far as his means go, and the remainder is levied on the whole village.'

In police as well as in revenue matters, the *patel* was under the superintendence of the *mamlatdár* (sub-collector), whose duty it was to see that all villages acted in concert, and with proper activity. His establishment of *sibandis* (irregular infantry) and *silladárs* (irregular cavalry) was employed to oppose violence and to support the village police, though not to detect offenders. With the *mamlatdár* also rested the general arrangements with the chiefs of Bhíls and other predatory tribes, either for abstaining from plunder themselves, or for assisting to check plunder in others. The *mamlatdár* had great discretionary powers; and even a *patel* would not hesitate to arrest a suspected person, or to take any measure that seemed necessary to preserve the peace of his village, for which he was answerable.

Such was the Marátha system of police that prevailed throughout the Deccan, except in the great towns, which had an organisation of their own under *kotwáls* (chief constables). It was, of course, liable to abuses, which had become particularly rife under the weak government of Báji Báo. But, on the whole, it did not work badly, particularly when contrasted with the condition of Bengal, as revealed in a then recent Parliamentary inquiry. There, one of the indirect consequences of the introduction of Lord Cornwallis's system had been to destroy the executive authority both of the *zamíndárs* and of the village watch; while English officers and English courts were not yet numerous enough to make their influence felt among such an immense population. The result was a formidable recrudescence of *dákaití* (gang-robbery), which paralysed the arm of criminal justice for many years. Whereas, in the Deccan,

'the reports of the Collectors do not represent crimes as particularly numerous. Mr. Chaplin, who has the best opportunity of drawing a comparison with our old provinces [Madras], thinks them rather rarer here than there. Murder for revenge, generally arising either from jealousy or disputes about landed property and village rank, is mentioned as the commonest crime among the Maráthás. Arson and cattle-stealing, as a means of avenging wrongs or extorting justice, is common in the Carnatic. Gang robberies and highway robbery are common, but almost always committed by Bhíls and other predatory tribes, who scarcely form part of the society; and they have never, since I have been in the country, reached to such a pitch as to bear a moment's comparison with the state of Bengal described in the papers laid before Parliament.'

And this in face of a system of criminal justice that beggars description. There was no recognised code of law, and no prescribed form of trial. Judicial power was vested in the revenue officers, and varied with their rank—from the *patél*, who could only put a man for a few days in the village lock-up, to the more important *mamlatdárs*, who latterly had the power of life and death. A Jagírdár was held to have supreme authority over his own troops and servants, wherever he was. The right of inflicting punishment was, however, extremely undefined, and was exercised by each according to his power or influence rather than his office. The highest officials, if at Poona, would pay the Peshwa the attention of applying for his sanction in a capital case.

'A principal rebel, or a leader of banditti, would be executed at once, on the ground of notoriety; any Bhíl caught in a part of the country where the Bhíls were plundering the road, would also be hanged immediately. In doubtful cases, the chief authority would order some of the people about him to inquire into the affair. The prisoner was examined; and if suspicions were strong, he was flogged to make him confess. Witnesses were examined, and a summary of their evidence and of the statement of the accused was always taken down in writing. They were sometimes confronted with the accused, in the hope of shaming or perplexing the party whose statement was false; but this was by no means necessary to the regularity of the proceedings. . . . No law seems ever to have been referred to, except in cases connected with religion, where Shástrís [Hindu jurisprudents] were sometimes consulted. The only rule seems to have been the custom of the country, and the magistrate's notions of expediency. The Hindu law was quite disused, probably owing to its absurdity.

'Murder, unless attended with peculiar atrocity, appears never to have been capital. Highway robbery was generally punished with death, because it was generally committed by low people. A man of tolerable caste was seldom put to death, except for offences against the State. In such cases, birth seems to have been no protection. A brother of Holkar was trampled to death by an elephant for rebellion, or rather for heading a gang of predatory horse; a dispossessed Jagírdár was blown away from a gun for a similar offence. . . . The other capital punishments were hanging, beheading, cutting to pieces with swords, and crushing the head with a mallet. Bráhman prisoners, who could not be executed, were poisoned, or made away with by deleterious food. Women were never put to death; long confinement, and the cutting off the nose, ears, and breast was the severest punishment inflicted on them. Mutilation was very common. Hard labour, in building fortifications especially, was not unknown. . . . But the commonest of all punishments was fine and confiscation of goods, to which the *mamlatdár* was so much prompted by his avarice, that it is often difficult to say whether it was inflicted as the regular punishment, or merely made use of as a pretence for gaining wealth. On the one hand, it seems to have been the Marátha practice to punish murder, especially if committed by a man of good caste, by fine; but on the other, the *mamlatdárs* would frequently release Bhíl robbers, contrary to the established custom, and even allow them to renew their depredations on the payment of a sum of money. No other punishment, it may be averred, was ever inflicted on a man who could afford to pay a fine; and, on the whole, the criminal system of the Maráthás was in the last state of disorder and corruption.'

It was, of course, impossible for an English governor to continue this system; but Elphinstone introduced his reforms with scrupulous regard for native sentiments and prejudices. The *patél* was permitted only as much authority as would preserve his influence in his village. The powers of the *mamlatdár* were at first limited to a fine of two rupees and confinement for twenty-four hours, but afterwards augmented to allow of his punishing petty affrays. All other criminal jurisdiction, short of capital punishment, was vested in the Collector.

'According to our practice, a prisoner is formally and publicly brought to trial. He is asked whether he is guilty. If he admits it, pains are taken to ascertain that his confession is voluntary; if he denies it, witnesses are called without further inquiry. They are examined in the presence of the prisoner, who is allowed to cross-examine them, and to call witnesses in his own defence. If there is any doubt when the trial is concluded, he is acquitted; if he is clearly guilty, the Shástrí is called on to declare the Hindu law. It often happens that this law is unreasonable; and when the error is on the side of severity, it is modified; when on the side of lenity, it is acquiesced in. In Khándesh a regular jury is generally assembled, who question the witnesses and pronounce on the guilt of the accused. In Sátára the Political Agent calls in several respectable persons, besides the law officers, and benefits by their opinion, both in the conduct of the trial and in determining the verdict. When the trial is concluded and the sentence passed, in cases of magnitude it is reported for confirmation to the Commissioner, where the same leaning to the side of lenity is shown as in the court itself.'

Elphinstone admitted that this procedure—modelled on that of the courts in England—was better calculated for protecting the innocent and lightening the punishment of the guilty, than for securing the community by deterring from crime. In regard to certainty and efficacy of punishment, it had the same inferiority to the native system that the reformed police had in detecting and seizing offenders. Subsequent experience suggested to him various improvements. He recommended the cross-examination of the accused; since 'an innocent man cannot criminate himself, and it is well that a guilty man should do so.' He also thought that the magistrate should have the assistance of some intelligent natives of his own choosing at the trial; for 'their knowledge of the people would often lead to discoveries of the truth that might escape a European.' He would abolish all reference to the Hindu law, which was in reality an English innovation. 'Some of the Hindu punishments are too dreadful to be inflicted, others are too trifling to be of any use in deterring. The Shástrí at Ahmednagar sentenced one man to be thrown from a height upon a spike, and another to be fined six *fanams* for the same offence, because in one case the stolen property had been accidentally recovered, and in the other it had not.' But he would allow great weight to caste in allotting punishment, 'because an opposite conduct shocks the prejudices of the people, which unless we conciliate, all our justest sentences will be looked on as tyranny.'

The entire subject of punishments was reviewed

by Elphinstone, in the light of his recent study of Bentham.

'Our punishments, I should think, might be made more intense, but shorter: severe flogging, solitary confinement in dungeons for short periods, bad fare, severe labour, and similar punishments, always so guarded as to prevent their endangering life or health. Transportation seems a good punishment, provided it be for life; but the return of a convict destroys the mysterious horror which would otherwise be excited by the sentence. Hanging in chains would probably make a great impression, if not too shocking to the prejudices of the natives, which I apprehend it is not. As much form as possible should be thrown into all punishments, especially capital ones; and great care should be taken to suit the forms to the native ideas. They have themselves an excellent practice of exposing persons about to suffer death on a camel, stripped of some of their clothes, with their hair loose and covered with red powder and with flowers, as is usual with a corpse when carried to the funeral pyre. Some of the most terrible modes of capital punishment might be retained when they do not add to the sufferings of the criminal: beheading and blowing away from a gun are of this nature, but they ought to be reserved for great crimes. The opinions of natives ought, however, to be taken, and may be reckoned conclusive on subjects depending on feeling and on associations.'

On the subject of imprisonment, also, he made some far-sighted suggestions. He was struck, on the one hand, by the indifference with which natives regarded sentences of imprisonment, as inflicting on them no greater hardships than their ordinary life; and, on the other hand, by the impolicy of discharging altogether those whose innocence was more than doubtful. With reference to the latter class of cases, he wrote:

'Means might perhaps be found to manage the imprisonment of suspected persons in such a manner as to preserve the distinction between their treatment and that of convicts. Their place of confinement might be more like a workhouse than a prison. They might be taught trades and allowed the fruit of their own industry. . . . A place might be constructed for their residence which would combine the plan so much recommended by Bentham with the economical arrangement suggested in Bengal. [Here follows a sketch of a Panopticon adapted to Indian requirements.] Persons less suspected might be consigned to the care and responsibility of the *patéls* of their villages; and there are cases where wandering and thievish tribes might be compelled, on pain of imprisonment, to reside in particular villages, according to the plan recommended by General Munro.'

For any improvement in the general morals of the people Elphinstone looked solely to education, under which he included the use of the printing-press. He suggested the printing and cheap distribution of Hindu tales inculcating sound morals, and also religious books, if such could be found, tending more directly to the same end. But he recognised that the slightest infusion of religious controversy would cause the total failure of the plan. Here again the philosopher speaks:

'It would be better to call the prejudices of the Hindus to our aid in reforming them, and to control their vices by the ties of religion which are stronger than those of law. By maintaining and purifying their present tenets, at the same time that we enlighten their understandings, we shall bring them nearer to that standard of perfection at which all concur in desiring that they should arrive; while any attack on their faith, if successful, might be expected in theory, as is found in practice, to shake their reverence for all religion, and to set them free from those useful restraints which even a superstitious doctrine imposes on the passions.'

Elphinstone's report on the administration of civil justice supplies the most valuable evidence we possess as to the working of the primitive Hindu system, unaffected by Muhammadan law. Except in the great towns—where an official called the *nyáyádhish* tried causes in the Peshwa's name—no regular judges existed, the sole method of determining civil rights being the award of *pancháyats*, or councils of arbitration, summoned as occasion arose. *Panchayat* means literally 'a body of five,' though in practice it is not necessarily restricted to that number. Respect for its authority is one of the fundamental principles that hold together Hindu society, as may be gathered from the proverb—*Panchmen Parmeshwar*='God is with the Five.' After the death of Ranjít Singh, when all official authority in the Punjab disappeared, the army of the Khálsa reconstituted itself under elected *pancháyats*; and to this day *pancháyats* decide caste disputes throughout India, which often affect important issues of property or trade.

Elphinstone found the *pancháyat* in active operation in the Deccan, and did his best to preserve it, though he was well aware that it could not continue to exist after the introduction of English judges and English law. The essence of the system was the submission of the parties to an arbitration by their fellows, the whole proceeding being sanctioned by the presence of a Government official. If the parties were bankers, then the *panchayat* was composed of bankers; in the case of an ordinary dispute between villagers, the *patél* requested some of the most intelligent and impartial cultivators to meet him under a tree or in the temple. Every fiscal officer, from the *patél* to the *mamlatdár*, had the power to grant a *panchayat* on the application of the parties. In theory, the consent of both parties was necessary; but the plaintiff had effectual means of enforcing the consent of the defendant. For this purpose, as well as for the redress of other wrongs, recourse was had to the practice of *takáza*.

'If a man have a demand from [? upon] his inferior or his equal, he places him under restraint, prevents his leaving his house or eating, and even compels him to sit in the sun until he comes to some accommodation. If the debtor were a superior, the creditor had at first recourse to supplications and appeals to the honour and sense of shame of the other party: he laid himself on his threshold, threw himself on his road, clamoured before his door, or he employed others to do all this for him: he would even sit down and fast before the debtor's door, during which time the other was compelled to fast also, or he would appeal to the gods and invoke their curses upon the person by whom he was injured. It was a point of honour with the natives not to disturb the authors of these importunities, so long as they were just; and some satisfaction was generally procured by means of them. If they were unjust, the party thus harassed naturally concurred with the plaintiff in the wish for a *panchāyat*, and thus an object was obtained which might not have been gained from the indolence of the magistrate. Similar means were employed to extort justice from the ruling power: standing before the residence of the great man, assailing him with clamour, holding up a torch before him by daylight, pouring water without ceasing on the statues of the gods. These extreme measures seldom failed to obtain a hearing, even under Bájí Ráo; and there was the still more powerful expedient, both for recovering a debt or for obtaining justice, to get the whole caste, village, or trade, to join in performing the above ceremonies until the demands of one of its members were satisfied.'

When the attendance of the defendant had been obtained by some means or other, the first act of the meeting was to take a written acknowledgment of the consent of the parties. In the case of petty village disputes, two straws were given in token of submission, instead of a document.

'The plaintiff's complaint was then read, and the defendant's answer received; a replication and a rejoinder were sometimes added, and the parties were cross-questioned by the *panchāyat* as long as they thought it necessary.... A man might, if it were inconvenient for him to attend, send a *kárkun* [writer] in his service, or a relation; but the trade of a *rakíl* [law-agent] is not known. Accounts and other written evidence were called for after the examination of the parties, and likewise oral evidence when written failed; but a great preference was given to written documents. The witnesses seem to have been examined and cross-examined with great care; but the substance only of their evidence was taken down briefly without the questions, and generally in their own hand if they could write. . . . Oaths were seldom imposed, unless there were reason to suspect the veracity of the witness, and then great pains were taken to make them solemn. When this examination was concluded, the *panchayat*, after debating on the case, drew up an award, in which they gave the substance of the complaint and answer, an abstract of each of the documents presented on either side, a summary of the oral evidence, with their own decision on the whole. . . . In villages there was much less form: the *panchayat* was often conducted in the way of conversation, and nothing was written but the decision, and sometimes not even that. Throughout the whole proceedings, the *panchayats* appear to have been guided by their own notions of justice, founded no doubt on the Hindu law, and modified by the custom of the country. They consulted no books; and it was only on particular points immediately connected with the Hindu law, such as marriage or succession, that they referred to a Shástrí [jurisprudent] for his opinion. On the report of the *panchayat*, the officer of government proceeded to confirm and enforce its decree, the *panchayat* having no executive powers of its own. From this cause frequent references to the magistrate were required, and he was given a considerable influence on the progress of the trial.'

The faults in such a system of administering justice are self-evident—dilatoriness, want of executive power, exposure to corruption, and inability to deal with complicated issues. But, in Elphinstone's opinion, these faults were outweighed by greater advantages, especially for the decision of petty disputes. Above all, the interest of the people was enlisted in ascertaining and protecting their own rights, while litigiousness was not encouraged.

'The institution of *pancháyats* was a restraint on patronage and bribery. . . . The intimate acquaintance of the members with the subject in dispute, and in many cases with the characters of the parties, must have made their decisions frequently correct; and it was an advantage of incalculable value in this mode of trial that the judges, being drawn from the body of the people, could act on no principles that were not generally understood, a circumstance which, by preventing uncertainty and obscurity in the law, struck at the very root of litigation. . . . The *pancháyats* appear, even after the corrupt reign of Bájí Ráo, to have retained in a great degree the confidence of the people; and they do not appear to have been unworthy of their good opinion. All the answers to my queries (except those of one Collector) give them a very favourable character; and Mr. Chaplin, in particular, is of opinion that in most instances their statement of the evidence is succinct and clear, their reasoning on it solid and perspicuous, and their decisions just and impartial.'

Elphinstone, then, decided without much hesitation in favour of maintaining the system of *pancháyats*. The only alternative that he saw before him was the introduction of the Adálat (Civil Court); and to that he was strongly averse, not only because he knew how the natives dreaded it, but still more because he could not find any recognised code of civil rights for English judges to administer. In the following chapter some account will be given of the measures which Elphinstone adopted at Bombay to remove the latter difficulty. With regard to the former, he was content with the reflection that, if his reformed *panchayats* should fail, it would never be too late to introduce the Adálat.

His reforms aimed at reviving the energy and removing the abuses of the native system, while preserving all its main features. He even went so far as to tolerate the practice of *takáza*, upon which rested the primary sanction that compelled resort to the *panchayat*, though he permitted only such restraints and inconveniences as appeal to personal honour. He insisted that the *panchayats* should continue to be free from all forms and interference. Some pressure might be put upon the members to induce them to attend, and perhaps their attendance might be rewarded with a small fee. No papers should be required from them beyond the written consent of the parties and the written award, as concise as they chose to make it. When these papers could be produced, the decision should be final, except in case of corruption or gross injustice, when an appeal might be brought to the Collector. The function of the Collector was confined to granting a new *panchayat*, the object of this appeal being rather to watch over the purity of the courts than to amend their decisions. To discourage litigation, and frivolous appeals in particular, it was suggested that the *panchayat* or the presiding officer should have power to fine a party whose suit was palpably frivolous. Fees for judicial proceedings were disapproved by Elphinstone, on the Benthamite ground that 'it is very doubtful whether they are a check on litigation any farther than they are a check on justice.' Decrees should be enforced according to the mildest forms already in use. A messenger should be first sent to demand payment, by the threat of preventing the debtor from eating between sunrise and sunset. Next, the property of the debtor might be sold, but not his house or the implements of his calling. If this should be insufficient, he might be imprisoned, for a term to be fixed by the *panchâyat* according to the amount of his debt, and the fraudulent or vexatious spirit he had displayed.

Panchâyats were ordinarily to be granted, as they always had been, by *patéls* (head-men of villages) and *mamlatdârs* (deputy-collectors of districts), subject to the general superintendence of the English Collector. And Elphinstone was careful to insist that the Collector should not only make regular tours through his district, but should also give audience, for at least two hours every day, to all ranks, receive complaints *viva voce*, and grant decisions and orders against *mamlatdârs*, as the cases required. For while he liberally augmented the salary of the *mamlatdârs* and granted them other privileges, he saw that their integrity and efficiency could be preserved only by strict discipline. For the larger towns, a staff of *amíns* (native judges) was constituted, with power either to grant *panchâyats*, or to decide themselves complaints referred to them by the Collector, when both parties had consented to that mode of adjustment. The employment of professional *vakíls* (law-agents) was strictly forbidden in all courts alike.

Elphinstone thus concludes this branch of his Report:

'I hope the plan now proposed will be effectual. Should it fail, it will be necessary to have numerous *amíns* for holding *panchâyats*, and to adopt by degrees stricter rules to compel the attendance and hasten the decisions of those bodies. If that should be insufficient, *múnsífs* [subordinate judges] must be empowered to try causes by themselves, in which case there must be a European judge to hear appeals from them all. But these improvements must not be introduced until they are wanted; and we must be careful not to induce the natives to give up their present modes of settling disputes, by holding out a prospect of pure and abundant justice which we may not ultimately be able to realise.'

Elphinstone's settlement of the Deccan occupied him for little more than a year. His appointment as Commissioner dates from December, 1817; his proclamation, announcing that Bájí Ráo had forfeited his sovereignty, was issued in the following February. In March, he returned to Poona for the first time since the outbreak of hostilities, riding with an escort to protect him from the Peshwa's Pindárís.

'I am lodged at the palace and am now seated in the Peshwa's closet, where our first consultation about the proceedings took place; and I have been shutting the door the closing of which on the Séth [banker] probably first led to all subsequent misunderstandings. . . . Poona, when approached, is unchanged in appearance; but the destruction of all our houses destroys every feeling of quiet and home, and the absence of the Hindu government occasions a void that alters the effect of everything. Our respect for the place is gone, and the change is melancholy. How must the natives feel this when even we feel it!'

Elphinstone had no time for literature during this busy period. His reading seems to have been almost confined to Bentham, of which his friend Erskine sent him a copy — presumably the *Introduction to the Principles of Morals and Legislation*. On first looking into it, he was disposed to be critical; but this feeling quickly changed to respect and admiration. A few years later he was extremely flattered at receiving from Bentham himself a present of his books: 'I know no author from whom I should so highly have valued such a distinction. . . . He is certainly a man of first-rate talents, but also of first-rate eccentricity; which, both in his doctrines and his personal habits, probably arises from his little intercourse with the world.'

The Commissionership of the Deccan was, from its nature, a provisional appointment. Elphinstone hoped that he might complete his task in two years at the furthest, and then fulfil his long-deferred intention of visiting England. But in February, 1819, he learnt, with some surprise, that he had been selected by the Court of Directors to be Governor of Bombay. If we may trust the confessions committed to his diary, the honour did not unduly elate him. The failure of his mission to Kábul had cured him of Indian ambition; the hope of seeing his friends and relations at home had to be again indefinitely postponed; while he entertained doubts whether his health would permit

THE SETTLEMENT OF THE DECCAN 157

another protracted term of residence in India. He had been happy at Poona, where the climate, the country, and the people alike suited him. He dreaded the change to Bombay, with its new duties, strange society, and enervating atmosphere. Nevertheless, he went to his enlarged sphere of work in good heart, and with a serious resolution that he would at least deserve public approval. 'Justice is the basis of all esteem, and even of all permanent popularity. . . . . One grand rule is to avoid all promises, express or implied. Another, of more general extent, is not to court popularity directly, but to aim at the esteem of the public by study and able conduct.'

Before taking up office he appears to have contemplated a trip to Calcutta, in order to consult with Lord Hastings, who was still Governor-General. But this project was upset by an imperative call for his presence in the Southern Marátha country, which he had not yet visited. He went thither from Bombay on board the *Curlew*, a frigate originally built for the Imám of Muscat. He was landed at Malwán, the port in the Konkan which he had formerly rescued from pirates. Thence he proceeded by land to Goa, where he was received in state by the Portuguese Viceroy, and admitted into the disused dungeons of the Inquisition. In one cell he was shown a contrivance for listening unseen to the talk of the prisoners. He was struck by the marked signs of civilisation in the Old Territory. 'The good roads, the numerous enclosures, the comfortably tiled houses, the water-courses faced with stone and crossed by bridges—all spoke a European colony, as much as the churches and crosses.' From Goa he passed over the Gháts to Belgáum, the capital of the Maráthá Karnatik. It was here that he had his interview with Chintáman Ráo, the recalcitrant Jagírdár, which has already been mentioned[1]. Thence his route lay near Bijápur, the ruined capital of a great Muhammadan dynasty, and now (1891) the headquarters of a prosperous British district. As always, Elphinstone turned out of his way to inspect the ruins, the great dome of the mausoleum of Máhmúd Adíl Sháh having been his guide for nearly two days' march. He declares Bijápur to far surpass anything he had seen in the Deccan. In July, he returned to Poona, where he remained for three months, occupied with the constant drudgery of writing his Report. At last, in October, 1819, after many handsome entertainments, he bade farewell to the Deccan in the following characteristic words:

'I feel a sort of respect as well as attachment for this fine picturesque country, which I am leaving for the flat and crowded roads of Bombay; and I cannot but think with affectionate regret of the romantic scenes and manly sports of the Deccan :

> 'ὦ λύκοι, ὦ θῶες, ὦ ἀν' ὤρεα φωλάδες ἄρκτοι,
> χαίρεθ'· ὁ βωκόλος ὔμμιν ἐγὼ Δάφνις οὐκ ἔτ' ἀν' ὕλαν,
> οὐκ ἔτ' ἀνὰ δρυμώς, οὐκ ἄλσεα· χαῖρ' 'Αρέθοισα
> καὶ ποταμοί[2].'

---

[1] *Ante*, p. 130.   [2] THEOCR. *Id.* i. 115-118.

CHAPTER X

Governor of Bombay

1819—1827

THE circumstances of Elphinstone's appointment to Bombay were unusual. Canning, then President of the Board of Control, with whom the patronage really rested, had written a letter to the Court of Directors suggesting that the usual custom of nominating an English statesman should be departed from in the present case, which seemed to offer a fitting reward for the exceptional ability recently displayed by several of the Company's servants, and recommending that the selection should lie between Elphinstone, Malcolm, and Munro. The choice fell upon Elphinstone, though it appears that he was not supported by his own uncle among the Directors. Malcolm, who was the senior by some ten years, and who could undoubtedly point to a longer and more brilliant record of achievements, did not conceal his chagrin at being passed in the race. But not even this rivalry was allowed to interfere with their cordial friendship or the candour of their correspondence. They wrote to one another about the result as if some third person had been the winner. Elphinstone possessed the advantages of being a civilian by profession, and of not being conspicuously connected with the forward policy of Lord Wellesley, which had never been welcome to the Court of Directors. But the decisive consideration undoubtedly was the success with which he had already administered the Deccan, coupled with the desire that the new province should now be incorporated with the Presidency of Bombay under the control of the same guiding hand. Mr. Chaplin nominally succeeded him as Commissioner, but the supervision was henceforth exercised from Bombay, not from Calcutta.

Elphinstone's government of Bombay extended over precisely eight years, from November 1819, to November 1827. This was a period of peace in India, interrupted only by the First Burmese War, and by Lord Combermere's capture of Bhartpur, avenging the repulse of Lord Lake, and thus retrieving the last of the disasters which marked the reversal of Wellesley's policy. With Elphinstone, also, it was a time of tranquillity. Though scarcely in middle age, as the present generation reckons, and but half-way through his long life, he had already entered upon the final stage of his career. The activity and excitement, the ambitions and anxieties of youth lay behind him. With his character fixed by experience and reflection, and his bodily frame braced by exercise and abstinence, in the maturity of his intellectual powers, he could afford to enjoy the dignity and ease of his position. A mellow and fruitful autumn succeeded to an early spring and a forcing summer. Fate placed in his way no more opportunities for distinction. It is enough that he satisfied the expectations which had been formed from his appointment as the foremost member of the Indian service.

In a letter to his cousin, John Adam—whose death, a few years later, was a severe blow to him—Elphinstone thus comments on his new situation:

'Now, to answer your questions. How I like Bombay? Very well; and the first month, which you thought would be so disagreeable, better than I expect to like any future month. There were no troublesome forms and ceremonies, and much novelty and variety. The new and unknown details you allude to give me little trouble, as I have always Warden to tell me what is usual; and as to the new business not of detail, I like learning it. Besides, I am not nearly so hard-worked as in the Deccan, and much of my work (that is, much of what takes up my time) is half play, such as talking to people who come to me on business instead of puzzling over records or pumping natives, going to Council, going to church. What I dread, detest, and abhor, to a degree which I fancy never was equalled, is making speeches and ceremonies of that nature. . . . All the other people of Bombay harangue to such a degree that if I were Charles Fox, I should hold my tongue on purpose to put down the fashion. . . . Otherwise, the society is pleasant and easy. . . . The Governor, too, by the custom of Bombay, constantly drives out and is quite a private gentleman, which suits well with my habits and tastes. Now for the bad side. The climate, though pleasant enough at this season [December] must be dreadful in the hot weather. The rides, though beautiful, are confined. There is a great deal of trifling business and details with which a Government ought not to be plagued, because they bind it down to particulars, and prevent the general and constant superintendence, and the consideration of the past, the present and the future, which ought to be its essential duty. Another annoyance, inasmuch as it is a loss of time, is the Council. Ours is perfectly well-intentioned, good-humoured, and unanimous on great points; but of course they often differ on particular cases, and much time is lost in minute-writing. For instance, if a Collector applies for tents for his native establishment on a circuit of his district, I say "Granted;" but another member of the Government writes a minute to show that his case differs from Mr. So-and-so's case, in which tents were formerly allowed, and it takes half-an-hour to reply. On the other hand, the Councillors save a good deal of trouble, as I am able to refer to them matters which I do not understand myself.'

Compare the account of Elphinstone's life and habits given by John Warden, who knew him better than anyone else at this time:—

'During the eight years Mr. Elphinstone was Governor of Bombay he visited each part of the Presidency twice. I was with him as under-secretary during his last tour through the Peshwa's country. His habits, whether in the Presidency [Bombay city] or in the *mufassal* [the country] were the same. He rose at daybreak, and, mounting one of a large stud he always kept, rode for an hour-and-a-half, principally at a hard gallop. He had a public breakfast every morning, and never left the room as long as one man desirous of speaking to him remained; but after that he was invisible to all but his suite. I have been associated in the same relation with Sir John Malcolm, Lord Clare, Sir Robert Grant, and many good men of business; but Mr. Elphinstone was the best. His industry was such that he took as much pains about a matter of five rupees as with the draft of a treaty. He had the pen of a ready writer, his minutes being written off quickly and without erasure. After luncheon he took a short *siesta*, and in the afternoon read Greek or Latin. I have been called to him sometimes as late as six o'clock in the evening, and remained till there was only time left to stroll for half-an-hour before an eight o'clock dinner. At ten he rose from the table and, after reading for half-an-hour in his own room, went to bed. Although surrounded by young men, he never suffered the slightest indecorum; and if any one after dinner indulged in a *double entendre*, he would not say anything, but, pushing back his chair, broke up the party. We always had in the camp a *shikári* [huntsman] whose business it was to inquire for hog; and whenever he brought in intelligence of game, Mr. Elphinstone would proclaim a holiday, and go hunting for one or perhaps two days, and he was fond of a chase at any time. In the midst of many striking excellences, that which placed him far above all the great men I have heard of, was his forgetfulness of self and thoughtfulness for others.'

To complete the picture of Elphinstone as he appeared to men qualified to judge, we may quote the character of him given by Bishop Heber, who was his guest for some time in May, and again in August of 1825 [1].

'Mr. Elphinstone is, in every respect, an extraordinary man, possessing great activity of body and mind, remarkable talent for and application to public business, a love of literature and a degree of almost universal information, such

---

[1] *Narrative of a Journey through the Upper Provinces of India, from Calcutta to Bombay*, 1824-25. (Vol. ii. pp. 219, 220.)

as I have met with in no other person similarly situated, and manners and conversation of the most amiable and interesting character. While he has seen more of India and the adjoining countries than any man now living, and has been engaged in active political and sometimes military duties since the age of eighteen, he has found time not only to cultivate the languages of Hindustán and Persia, but to preserve and extend his acquaintance with the Greek and Latin classics, with the French and Italian, with all the elder and more distinguished English writers, and with the current and popular literature of the day, both in poetry, history, politics, and political economy. With these remarkable accomplishments, and notwithstanding a temperance amounting to rigid abstinence, he is fond of society; and it is a common subject of surprise with his friends in what hours of the day or night he finds time for the acquisition of knowledge. His policy, so far as India is concerned, appeared to me peculiarly wise and liberal; and he is evidently attached to and thinks well of the country and its inhabitants. His public measures, in their general tendency, evince a steady wish to improve their present condition. No government in India pays so much attention to schools and public institutions for education. In none are the taxes lighter; and in the administration of justice to the natives in their own languages, in the establishment of *pancháyats*, in the degree in which he employs the natives in official situations, and the countenance and familiarity which he extends to all the natives of rank who approach him, he seems to have reduced to practice almost all the reforms which had struck me as most required in the system of government pursued in those provinces of our Eastern empire which I had previously visited. His popularity (though to such a feeling there may be individual exceptions) appears little less remarkable than his talents and acquirements; and I was struck by the remark I once heard, that "all other public men had their enemies and their friends, but of Mr. Elphinstone everybody spoke highly."'

Elphinstone's government of Bombay was not marked by any of those conspicuous incidents which find a record in history. Beyond the frontier, there was fighting in the Persian Gulf. An officer employed there in the suppression of piracy, who had imprudently ventured some distance inland, was overwhelmed by a charge of desert Arabs, whose tactics recall recent memories of the Soudán. A new expedition was sent with better success, and this was followed up by other measures to promote trade. But it was announced that the British Government would take no part in the disputes of the Arab States, its interests being confined to the extirpation of piracy. At about the same time another naval expedition was despatched from Bombay to Mocha, in the Red Sea, to avenge an outrage on a marine officer, and to secure protection for the Company's factory there in the future. Within the geographical limits of India, Sind was still an independent State, governed by its own Amírs, who seem to have been more peaceably disposed than the frontier chieftains nominally under British control. As Elphinstone sagely remarked, 'some little depredation you must have on the borders of an Asiatic empire.'

During his first two years, Elphinstone paid two visits to Gujarát, in order to settle pressing political questions. The British districts caused comparatively little trouble, though his reports upon them are still valuable historical documents. The great fertility of the soil, together with the security of British peace, lightened the burden even of a high assessment. The jurisdictions of the Collectors were small, and considerable latitude was allowed to them; for Bombay has never had a Board of Revenue, and there was then no Commissioner for Gujarát. The question of the Adálats (Civil Courts) naturally attracted Elphinstone's attention; and he was surprised to find them, on the whole, so little unpopular. He does, indeed, mention two grievances, both characteristic of a period of transition. In his report on Kaira, he remarks that one Rájá, who in 1804 maintained a body of 150 horse and 2000 foot, had been sent to prison for neglecting a summons from a magistrate; and that another Chief, who once resisted for two months the attack of the Gáekwár's army, was thrown into gaol for his inability to pay debts contracted during his independence and in consequence of war.

'I cannot more strongly show the change that has taken place than by pointing out that these are the persons whom Colonel Walker, and I believe all the gentlemen employed in the first introduction of our authority, declared to be sovereign princes, with whom we have no right to interfere beyond the collection of a tribute, and that they are now deprived of all power and consequence, and nearly the whole of their revenue. Almost all these changes have, in effect, taken place within these three years. They cannot but feel a change so sudden; and it must be owned that they have suffered hardships, though not perhaps injustice.'

Again, he comments upon the complaints of the cultivators that they were rendered liable, through the Adálats, for debts contracted under the Marátha government.

'The root of the grievance seems to lie in the readiness with which a bond is admitted as a sufficient evidence of the justice of a claim. In this case it is by no means so; for a *ráyat* is easily drawn by occasional advances and partial payments into a complicated account which it is impossible for him to unravel. This account presents a great balance in the lender's favour; and as the practice is for the *ráyat* to give up his produce each year in part payment, and to take an advance to enable him to go on with the next, he is so completely in the lender's power that he would sign anything rather than disoblige him. The remedy, therefore, is to settle that in new provinces a bond shall not be conclusive when originating in an old debt of a *ráyat*, but that his whole account shall be examined as if no bond had been executed, and only the amount which shall then appear fair decreed to the plaintiff. If the debts could be paid by instalments regulated by the amount of the *ráyat's* payments to Government, it would complete the removal of the evil; but, at all events, steps should be taken to prohibit the sale of a *ráyat's* cattle and implements of husbandry in satisfaction of debts.'

Two other practical reforms (mentioned by Bishop Heber) were also introduced by Elphinstone at about this time: the seat of the Adálat was moved from Bombay to Surat, in the heart of Gujarát; and Gujaráthí was substituted for Persian as the official language of the court.

The numerous Native States that form the external

fringe of Gujarát presented more difficulty. The overthrow of the Peshwa had not only brought the Deccan under British rule, it had also made the Company inheritor of all the ill-defined authority which he used to exercise in Gujarát as head of the Marátha power. In some cases, large tracts of territory were subdivided in varying proportions between the Peshwa and the Gáekwár; in others, semi-independent chiefs paid tribute to both. The settlement of these questions was rendered more easy by the weakness of the Baroda government. Ever since the Gáekwár accepted the subsidiary system in 1802, there had been a long regency, during which supreme authority was practically vested in the British Resident. Advantage was taken of this condition of affairs to consolidate the power of the Gáekwár within his own dominions, and at the same time to curtail his exactions from his feudatories, who were in many cases feudatories also of the Company. Both in the peninsula of Káthiáwár, and in the hilly and wild tract known as the Máhí Kántha, a settlement was effected, by which the tribute due to the Gáckwár was permanently fixed, and was to be paid to him through British officers. This arrangement continues to the present time.

One of Elphinstone's first duties was to proceed to Baroda, and to install the new Gáekwár, Syájí Ráo, to whom full power over his own dominions was restored. According to Bishop Heber, who visited him four years later, he turned out a fairly satisfactory prince, his worst fault being avarice. His revenue, even in those days, was reckoned at £800,000; and Heber thought him probably the most powerful personage in India after Ranjít Singh. It is interesting to learn that three sons of the murdered Shástrí were then occupying high positions at his court.

Elphinstone also visited Cutch, which was likewise under a regency, owing to the crimes and intolerable misrule of the Ráo. Here the troubles came from two sources. On the one hand, the country had recently suffered from a terrible earthquake, which shook down towns and castles, and permanently modified some of the physical features. On the other hand, anarchy had led to constant border troubles with the inhabitants of Sind; while the constitution of the State made it particularly difficult to suppress disorders. In theory, supreme power was shared with the Ráo by all his kinsmen of the Jareja clan of Rájputs, whose number Elphinstone puts at 200. With regard to them he wrote:

'The three most probable points of difference with the Jarejas are: settling their disputes among themselves; enforcing the prohibition of female infanticide; and compelling them to act against plunderers within their own districts. In the first, all danger may be averted by the prompt and impartial administration of justice; in the second, by caution and delicacy in the means of detecting guilt and moderation in punishing it. The third is an object of great importance. It is more likely to be attained by vigilance than by severity, by explaining what is expected, censuring neglect, and compelling restitution, with the addition of a fine as the punishment of participation. Great care should be taken to avoid any appearance of arrogance in our treatment of the Jareja chiefs; but I do not think there is any necessity for referring political questions to the decision of their body to the extent which a superficial view of the correspondence of the Residency would lead us to think usual.'

The peninsula of Káthiáwár had been settled by Colonel Walker in 1805. His method was to classify according to jurisdiction some 300 different chiefs, each of whom claimed to be sovereign and independent within his own territory, though their revenues varied from £120,000 to £10 a year, and they all paid tribute to the Gáekwár or to the Company as the heir of the Peshwa.

'Formerly they were constantly engaged in wars among themselves, and liable to the annual devastation of a Marátha army. . . . They are now quite peaceable, but circumstances have prevented their being prosperous. Famine, the plague, the cholera, and the incursions of marauders from Cutch and the desert have carried off a third of the population, and left almost all the chiefs in debt and difficulty.'

As the only means of securing the tribute, it had been proposed to supersede almost all the chiefs for a term of ten or twelve years, farming their lands, and reserving to them a pecuniary allowance. To Elphinstone this seemed too drastic a remedy. He was content to take from them a temporary assignment of a portion of their lands, sufficient to guarantee the payment of a portion of the tribute. It was many years before Káthiáwár recovered its prosperity; but at the present time several of its chiefs are among the most enlightened rulers in India, with a contented people and a full treasury.

Máhí Kántha gave rise to more perplexing problems than Káthiáwár. British control had been introduced as recently as 1813; but, as a matter of fact, the wild Bhíls and Kolís and the scarcely less wild Rájputs, who composed the population, were still unsubdued and refused to pay any tribute at all. It is curious to learn that the chiefs ranked in dignity according to the number of bowmen they could bring into the field. They numbered altogether 121, of whom 63 owed tribute to the Company and 24 to the Gáekwár, and one at least was a feudatory of Sindia. To add to the complication, many of the chiefs had claims to tribute upon each other; while some were further entitled to pecuniary grants (*giras*) arising out of lands in the possession of the Company or the Gáekwár. In truth, the problems to be adjusted were very similar to those which Malcolm was successfully dealing with in Central India. Elphinstone's first measures were to enforce order by a strong military force, to fix all liabilities still remaining indefinite, and to exact securities from the chiefs for the payment of tribute and the observance of their engagements in the future. These engagements included the following articles: to abstain from private war and from maintaining foreign mercenaries; to refer all disputes to the arbitration of the British Government; to give up plundering, and to apprehend and surrender plunderers ; to protect the passage of merchants, and to accept compensation for the privilege of levying transit duties ; and to prevent illicit trade in opium.

Though Gujarát occupied more of Elphinstone's attention, he was not altogether free from political trouble in the Deccan. The large State of Kolhápur, under a younger branch of the house of Sivají, was the focus of disorder, arising first from a long minority, and then from the arbitrary disposition of the young Rájá. Elphinstone was compelled to occupy his territory with troops, and to impose a minister upon him temporarily. Still stronger measures were adopted later by Elphinstone's successor. The story of the outbreak at Kittur shows that Elphinstone could act with severity when circumstances required it. Kittur was a small principality in the Southern Marátha country, under a Desái, whose *sanad* (patent) expressly limited the descent to lineal heirs. On the death of the Desái, in October, 1824, some prominent men in the State attempted to set up an adopted son. Elphinstone instructed Mr. Chaplin, Commissioner of the Deccan, to assume temporary charge of the State, pending an inquiry into the relationship of the person adopted. If it should appear that he was descended from the founder of the family, then Elphinstone announced that he would be content to waive any irregularity in the form of the adoption. But when Mr. Thackeray, assistant to Mr. Chaplin, reached Kittur with a small force, the gates were shut in his face.

An attack was repulsed; Thackeray was killed, and two British officers (one of whom was afterwards known to fame as Sir Walter Elliot) were taken prisoners. On hearing of this disaster, Elphinstone hurried up to Poona, put in motion an overwhelming body of troops to overawe the insurgents, and issued a proclamation declaring that the principality had passed under British rule in consequence of the extinction of the Desái's family, and offering a pardon to all rebels (except the principals) who should surrender by a certain date. This policy was successful. The English prisoners were well treated, and ultimately released without further fighting. In passing final judgment on the ringleaders, Elphinstone expressed his opinion that they had acted in ignorance of the relations existing between Kittur and the British Government.

What, however, caused Elphinstone more annoyance than these political troubles was his strained relations with the King's judges, which form almost a repetition of the historic quarrel between Warren Hastings and Sir Elijah Impey. A Supreme Court, consisting of a Chief Justice and Puisnes nominated by the Crown, was established at Bombay in 1823, in substitution for the Recorder's court, of which Sir James Mackintosh had been the most distinguished ornament. This must be carefully distinguished from the High Court, whose judges were servants of the Company, exercising both civil and criminal jurisdiction throughout the Presidency; whereas the authority of the Supreme Court

was supposed to be limited to the city of Bombay.
From their first arrival the new judges seem to have
claimed for themselves a position independent of, if
not superior to, that of the Governor and Council,
and to have viewed with suspicion every act of the
executive. Some of the occasions of dispute are too
petty to mention, but two of them rise to the rank of
constitutional questions.

One was connected with the freedom of the press.
A Regulation or statute had been passed by the
Supreme Government of India, substituting a set of
restrictions in place of the former censorship. No
Regulation was at that time valid within the Presidency towns until it had been first registered at the
Supreme Court. When Elphinstone, in accordance
with express orders from the Court of Directors,
offered the press statute for registration, the judges
claimed the right to determine as to its expediency,
and finally rejected it as not required. This led to a
wordy combat, at first carried on between the two
rival newspapers of Bombay, but afterwards continued
by the Chief Justice and Elphinstone himself. This
particular cause of quarrel was the more ridiculous,
as only a few months previously the Governor had
felt himself bound to deport an editor for reflections
on the judges. The circumstances are thus told by
Elphinstone in a letter to his friend Strachey, who now
occupied a high official position in the India House.

'Our Chief Justice quarrelled with the whole bar, and
formed a strong party against him in the society. One of

the newspapers belonging to that party published reports by members of the bar, which the Chief Justice complained of in March last [1824] as reflecting upon him. Warning was given to both the editors on that occasion; but in August the Chief Justice complained that he was attacked as usual. Threats were then addressed to the editor complained of, who was told that he would be sent home if he again offended. Next day he did again offend by an attack on the second Judge. Instead of being sent home, he was required to apologise; he would not, and he was sent home. The truth is he was before under orders from the Court of Directors to be sent home unless a licence arrived for him by a certain day, which had elapsed. He had no profession in this country but that of editor, and the proprietors could turn him off if he submitted; while, from their wealth and interest, they could also provide for him if he went home. Home, therefore, he was willing to go; and as the law required that he should be sent by a Company's ship, it was necessary to send him by China (no ships go direct) in the only ship that was to sail for nine or ten months. He was told, however, that he might stay for three months, if he would give security for going then, or when called on. This he refused, pretending that the security was excessive, though it did not signify if it had been for a hundred millions, unless he meant to break his pledge and stay beyond the time. By these means he got up a tolerably hard case, and had nearly got a harder by going home a charter-party passenger, when the Government cut him out of that advantage by paying 700 rupees (£70) for his passage at the cuddy table. To sum up: as there were Regulations, it was necessary to enforce them; and as the other party would make no concession, it was necessary to proceed to extremes. Not being particularly cordial with the Judges, I felt it more my duty to support them, as the belief that they were deserted by the Government would have emboldened their enemies. But, even at the best of times, I could not have turned a deaf ear to their complaints.'

It should be stated that Elphinstone was a consistent supporter of restrictions upon newspapers in India, which in those days meant, of course, English newspapers. He always had present to his mind the instability of the empire, and he was averse to incurring any unnecessary risk by encouraging criticism and consequent excitement. Bishop Heber remarks that Elphinstone's 'opinion and experience are the strongest presumptions which I have yet met with in favour of the censorship.' The press in India was not declared free until ten years later, in the brief Governor-Generalship of Metcalfe.

The other serious collision with the Supreme Court arose on a point of public law, which still possesses practical importance. During the war of 1817–18, a commandant of one of the Peshwa's forts carried away with him, in violation of the terms of his surrender, a large amount of treasure to Poona. There he was seized by Elphinstone's orders; some part of the treasure was found in his possession, and more was paid over by him before his release. He always claimed the treasure, either part or the whole, as his private property, but took no steps to prosecute the claim. After his death, a native banker at Bombay, to whom he had bequeathed his rights, brought an action of trover against Elphinstone personally in the Supreme Court.

'The want of jurisdiction of the court in a question of prize occurring before peace was quite restored, and in a country subject to the Supreme Government, was urged, as well as the danger of setting afloat all questions connected with the first settlement of a new conquest; but all were over-ruled. When the cause came on, the counsel for the plaintiff declaimed against the Government in the most unmeasured terms, promising to dispel the illusion under which the natives laboured, to expose the misgovernment of the Company, and to prevent the renewal of the Charter. The Judges listened with favour, the trial was protracted for twenty-one days, and every attempt made to bring out facts unfavourable to the Government.'

In the course of these proceedings, the court granted a subpoena against the Chief Secretary to produce all the records of the Government connected with the Marátha war. Supported by the opinion of the Advocate-General, Elphinstone declined to comply with the order. He was willing to furnish every paper that could throw light on the cause—indeed, every one where it was mentioned, with the exception of two secret despatches the disclosure of which might throw light on the channels through which intelligence was received. But as to the claim that the entire mass of records should be produced, he advised resistance, even if the court should go so far as to commit the Secretary for contempt.

'There must, I should think, be papers containing suspicions of the fidelity of particular powers; indications of the points in which our own Government is vulnerable; political plans not yet accomplished; several communications from individuals who would be injured by their publication; and many other papers which it would be a breach of duty in us to make known. On this ground, therefore, I would object to the records being furnished; but I would also do so on general principle, if I had no particular reason to think the publication of the records would be hurtful in this instance. If the records of every department are once placed at the mercy of every attorney who makes an application to the Supreme Court, there can be no secrecy in any affair, foreign or domestic, and no confidence in our own deliberations or in the persons with whom we have to communicate in any transaction.'

Elphinstone's biographer professes himself ignorant of the final issue of this affair. As a matter of fact, a verdict passed against Elphinstone in the Supreme Court for rupees 1,754,290 (£175,429); but this was set aside by the Privy Council, on appeal. A full report of the case is to be found in the second volume of the new series of State Trials, which is now being published under authority. It may be added that the conflict between the executive and the judicial power at Bombay reached its climax a few years later, under another Governor and another Chief Justice.

Hitherto we have only recounted episodes in the course of Elphinstone's administration of Bombay. But there are three subjects to which his continual attention was devoted, and upon which his fame as a Ruler of India rests: the codification of the law, the liberal admission of the natives to office, and the education of the people.

Even while at Poona Elphinstone had studied Bentham, and had pondered over the possibility of drawing up a digest of the law as it stood at the time of the conquest. It was only after this was accomplished that he could contemplate the gradual substitution of English courts for the indigenous *pancháyats*. In a letter of that time he writes to Strachey, himself a jurist:

'The written law was that of the Hindus, always vague and unknown to the bulk of the people, often absurd and still oftener entirely disused. The unwritten law was composed of the maxims that occur to people of common sense in a country not remarkably enlightened, modified by Hindu law and Hindu opinions, and constantly influenced by the direct and lawful interference of the prince, who was fountain of all law, and by the weight of rank and wealth and interest.'

And again in a letter to Erskine, from whom he had learned his Benthamism:

'The first thing to do is to learn what the existing institutions are; and this, when there is no written law (none that is acted on at least) must be a work of time. No one man or number of men can present in one view all the numerous customs and traditions that compose the actual law of this country. They will tell [you] what the Hindu law is, but it is never practised; or they will tell you of the practice in Bájí Ráo's time, when everything was venal. It is only by degrees, and as questions arise of themselves, that you get the answers and learn what mode of proceeding is generally esteemed lawful. The same sort of experience will suggest the parts of the system that require to be improved, and will help to point out the remedy. I think at the end of a year from this time there may be grounds for forming a confident opinion as to the best mode of administering justice.'

Within a year, Elphinstone had been transferred to Bombay, where one of the first acts of his administration was to appoint a committee for the codification of the law. One of the members of this committee was Erskine; the president was Babington, another ardent Benthamite. Their task was twofold: (1) To revise and reduce to system the existing Regulations or statutes passed by the Bombay Council; and (2) to investigate thoroughly the legal customs and usages of the people. The first and easiest portion of the task was satisfactorily accomplished. The Regulations dealt for the most part with matters of procedure, governing the constitution of the courts, fiscal, civil, and criminal; they also laid down some prohibitions and punishments, and settled a few questions of substantial law—such as the relations of master and servant, landlord and tenant—which forced themselves on the attention of Government from time to time. The revised Bombay Regulations, which came into effect in 1827, have received the following commendation from Sir James Stephen[1]. After speaking of the rough-and-ready codes framed by Lord Lawrence for the Punjab, he goes on:

'He was not, however, the first Indian statesman who had set an example in this direction. Mountstuart Elphinstone, when Governor of Bombay, had done a great and important work of the same kind. Under his administration the whole of the Bombay Regulations were formed into a

[1] *Sessional Proceedings of the National Association for the Promotion of Social Science for* 1872-3 (p. 8).

code, regularly arranged according to their subject-matter. This code consists of twenty-seven Regulations, subdivided into chapters and sections. It refers to the same subjects as the Bengal Regulations, but differs from them in the circumstance that it contains a body of substantial criminal law which remained in force until it was superseded by the Criminal Code, and which had very considerable merits, though it would probably not have supported the test of strict professional criticism, to which indeed it was not intended to be subjected.'

The other portion of the work of the committee was that in which Elphinstone himself took most interest, though no results were produced commensurate with the labour expended. A digest of Hindu law is even at the present day beyond the hope of Indian law reformers. But Elphinstone's original design went much further. It is one of his chief merits to have laid down—what is not yet generally recognised— that 'what we call Hindu law applies to the Bráhmans only: each caste has separate laws and customs of its own, and even these vary according to the part of the country in which the different portions of a caste are settled.' On the other hand, his experience of Gujarát taught him a better opinion of our Civil Courts, though he never wavered in his belief that the *zamíndárí* system of Cornwallis had destroyed the police system and hopelessly injured the status of the *ráyats* in Bengal. The object, therefore, that he kept constantly in view was the preparation of a complete code of Hindu civil law, based partly upon the written books and partly upon the existing customs, which should be administered generally by the English courts. His plan is thus formulated in a Minute dated July, 1823.

'The Dharma Shástra, it is understood, is a collection of ancient treatises neither clear nor consistent in themselves, and now buried under a heap of more modern commentaries, the whole beyond the knowledge of perhaps the most learned *pandits*, and every part wholly unknown to the people who live under it. Its place is supplied in many cases by known customs, founded indeed on the Dharma Shástra, but modified by the convenience of different castes or communities, and no longer deriving authority from any written text. The uncertainty of all decisions obtained from such sources must be obvious, especially when required for the guidance of a foreign judge, himself a stranger both to the written law and to the usage which in cases supplies its place. The usual resource, when the Shástra has to be consulted, is to refer to the *pandit* of the court, on whose integrity the justice of the decision must in the first instance depend. Supposing, however, that he is honest and learned (which last quality is not now common, and must daily become more rare), he has the choice of a variety of books to quote from, and in many instances the same book has a variety of decisions on the same question. When the question depends on customs, the evil is at least as great. The law is then to be collected from the examinations of private individuals; the looseness of tradition must lead to contrary opinions; and even when any rule is established, it is likely to be too vague to be easily applied to the case in point. Add to this the chance of corruption, faction-favour, and other sources of partiality among witnesses.

'There are but two courses by which a remedy can be

applied. The first is to make a new code founded entirely on general principles, applicable to all ages and nations. The second is to endeavour to compile a complete and consistent code from the mass of written law and the fragments of tradition, determining on general principles of jurisprudence those points where the Hindu books and traditions present only conflicting authorities, and perhaps supplying on similar principles any glaring deficiencies that may remain when the matter for compilation has been exhausted. The first of these courses, if otherwise expedient, is rendered entirely impracticable here by the attachment of the natives to their own institutions, and by the degree to which their laws are interwoven with their religion and manners. The second plan, is, therefore the only one which it is in our power to pursue. The first step towards the accomplishment of its objects appears to be to ascertain in each district whether there is any book of acknowledged authority, either for the whole or any branch of the law. The next is to ascertain what exceptions there are to the written authorities, and what customs and conditions exist independent of them. The best modes of conducting these inquiries are—first, to examine the Shástris, heads of castes, and other persons likely to be acquainted either with the law, the custom of castes, or the public opinion regarding the authority attached to each; and, second, to extract from the records of the courts of justice the information already obtained on these subjects in the course of judicial investigation.'

This Minute was written exactly ten years before the appointment of the Law Commission of 1833, of which Macaulay was the most prominent member. The Penal Code, drafted by that Commission, did not become law until 1860. A long series of other codes have since been approved by the Indian legislature[1], dealing with such special subjects as contracts, trusts, negotiable instruments, &c. The civil and criminal procedure has also been codified. But Elphinstone's project of reducing to intelligible form the entire body of Hindu law and custom, both written and unwritten, still remains unaccomplished, being as far in advance of our time as it was of his. The only immediate results were the compilation of a work by Mr. Steele, giving a mass of information regarding rules of caste, marriage, inheritance, &c.; a series of reports of decisions of the courts of law, prepared by Mr. Borradaile ; and a translation of a Sanskrit book on inheritance by the same author. None of these works, however, appeared until the year in which Elphinstone left Bombay, and then the scheme was dropped.

With regard to the admission of natives to office, Elphinstone's views were not less in advance of his time. These views were maintained by him consistently from the time of his early administration at Poona down to the day of his death. They were not suggested by sentiment, but based upon the broadest principles of political philosophy. It is possible that Elphinstone received his first impulse in this direction from the genial nature of Malcolm and from the mature wisdom of Munro. He always wrote in admiration of Malcolm's sympathetic treatment of the natives ; and he was ever ready to learn

[1] See *The Anglo-Indian Codes*. Edited by Whitley Stokes. (Two vols., 1887 and 1888, with Supplements for 1890 and 1891.)

from Munro how they might be safely entrusted with
larger administrative powers. His own experience as
Commissioner of the Deccan taught him the importance, and also the difficulty, of carrying his theories
into practice. Meanwhile, his reading—especially of
Bentham and of books about China—and his intercourse with Mackintosh and Erskine, had led him to
form speculative opinions upon the future of British
rule, which would sound very advanced even at the
present day. As the deliberate conviction of the
most enlightened mind that has devoted itself to the
government and history of India, Elphinstone's pro-
phetic forecast seems hardly to have attracted the
attention it deserves.

As early as May, 1819, while still in the Deccan, he
wrote to Malcolm:

'Sooner or later, it is probably desirable that we should
have all the country... If we can then manage our native
army, and keep out the Russians [1], I see nothing to threaten
the safety of our empire, until the natives become enlightened
under our tuition, and a separation becomes desirable to
both parties.'

In a letter to Mackintosh of the following month,
he speaks out yet more freely:

'I am afraid the belief that our Indian Empire will not
be long-lived is reason, and not prejudice. It is difficult to
guess the death it may die; but if it escapes the Russians,
and other foreign attacks, I think the seeds of its ruin will

[1] Observe that it is no longer the French who are the cause of anxiety.

be found in the native army—a delicate and dangerous machine, which a little mismanagement may easily turn against us. The most desirable death for us to die of should be, the improvement of the natives reaching such a pitch as would render it impossible for a foreign nation to retain the government; but this seems at an immeasurable distance.... A time of separation must come; and it is for our interest to have an early separation from a civilised people, rather than a violent rupture with a barbarous nation, in which it is probable that all our settlers and even our commerce would perish, along with all the institutions we had introduced into the country.'

On the occasion of the mutiny at Barrackpur (1826), he writes to Metcalfe in less desponding tones:

'I used to think our empire made of glass; but when one considers the rough usage it has stood, both in old times and recent, one is apt to think it is made of iron. I believe it is of steel, which cuts through everything if you keep its edge even, but it is very apt to snap short if it falls into unskilful hands.'

Nor were these speculations confined to private correspondence. They were convictions which Elphinstone did his best to carry out in practical administration, and which he ventured to incorporate in his official minutes. In his Report on the Deccan (1819), from which many quotations have already been made, he advocated the creation of posts for natives with a salary of not less than £1200 a year, on the ground that 'economy, no less than policy, requires liberal pay when there is considerable trust—a maxim long since confirmed in its application to the natives by the experience and sagacity of General Munro.' One of his first plans at Bombay (1820) — which was thwarted by the opposition of his colleagues in Council — was to graft a native college on the proposed European one, so as to educate native instruments of government by the side of young civil servants, and likewise to preserve and encourage native learning. Two years later (1822), on hearing that Munro had instituted something like a Native Board of Revenue at Madras, he writes to him for particulars:

'It seems to be one great advantage of the arrangement that it opens a door to the employment of natives in high and efficient situations. I should be happy to know if you think the plan can be extended to the judicial or any other line. Besides the necessity for having good native advisers in governing natives, it is necessary that we should pave the way for the introduction of the natives to some share in the government of their own country. It may be half a century before we are obliged to do so; but the system of government and education which we have already established must, some time or other, work such a change on the people of this country that it will be impossible to confine them to subordinate employments; and if we have not previously opened vents for their ambition and ability, we may expect an explosion which will overturn our government.'

And again, in 1826, in a letter to Henry Ellis—suggested by some public proposals of his in favour of the admission of natives to all offices—he writes:

'It has always been a favourite notion of mine that our object ought to be to place ourselves in the same relation to the natives that the Tartars are in to the Chinese: retaining the government and military power, but gradually relinquishing all share in the civil administration, except that degree of control which is necessary to give the whole an impulse and direction. This operation must be so gradual that it need not even alarm the Directors (as you suppose) for their civil patronage; but it ought to be kept in mind, and all our measures ought to tend to that object. The first steps are to commence a systematic education of the natives for civil offices, to make over to them at once a larger share of judicial business, to increase their emoluments generally, and to open a few high prizes for the most able and honest among them. The period when they may be admitted into Council (as you propose) seems to be distant; but they might very safely be consulted on all topics not political, and where there were no secrets to keep and no places to dispose of.'

Finally, no less radical views are to be found in a Minute on Education (1824), which was undoubtedly intended to come under the eyes of the Court of Directors:

'If care were taken to qualify the natives for the public service, and afterwards to encourage their employment, the picture would soon be reversed. At no very distant day we might see natives engaged in superintending a portion of a district as the European Assistants are now. In a more advanced stage, they might sometimes be Registrars and Sub-collectors, or even Collectors and Judges; and it may not be too visionary to suppose a period at which they might bear to the English nearly the relation which the Chinese do to the Tartars, the Europeans retaining the government and the military power, while the natives filled a large portion of the civil stations, and many of the subordinate employments in the army.

'It may be urged that, if we raise the natives to an equality with ourselves by education, and at the same time admit them to a share in their own government, it is not likely they will be content with the position assigned to them, or will ever rest until they have made good their title to the whole. It cannot be denied that there is much ground for the apprehension, but I do not see that we are at all more secure on any other plan. If we endeavour to depress the natives, our government may be overthrown by their resistance; and such a catastrophe would be more disastrous and more disgraceful than that just supposed. Even if we succeeded in the attempt, our empire, being unconnected with the people, would be liable to be subverted either by foreign conquest or by the revolt of our descendants; and it is better for our honour and interest, as well as for the welfare of mankind, that we should resign our power into the hands of the people for whose benefit it is entrusted, than that it should be wrested from us by a rival nation, or claimed as a birthright by a handful of creoles.

'These speculations may seem to be pushed too far, and they are certainly not proportioned to the limited question which has given rise to them. But it is necessary to fix on some system towards which our measures should be directed, since it is impossible to make a good choice of the means until we have come to a determination as to the end to be attained. If it is not thought desirable that the natives should at some future period be admitted to a share in the administration of the government, it would be highly impolitic and inconsistent to take even these partial measures for their improvement, or to retard their progress to a state of depression in which alone they can be expected to reconcile themselves to the station for which they are destined.'

Nearly thirty years later (1850), Elphinstone ex-

pressed identically the same opinions in a letter to
Charles Hay Cameron, suggested by the refusal of the
Court of Directors to appoint a qualified native to
the covenanted medical service[1]. In 1854 again, in
reference to a book about China, he wrote to Sir T. E.
Colebrooke, his biographer:

> 'The moral is that we must not dream of perpetual posses
> sion, but must apply ourselves to bring the natives into a
> state that will admit of their governing themselves in a
> manner that may be beneficial to our interest as well as their
> own and that of the rest of the world; and to take the
> glory of the achievement and the sense of having done our
> duty for the chief reward of our exertions.'

Nor was Elphinstone's deliberate judgment modified
one whit by the disturbing events of the Mutiny. In
the very year (1858) before his death, when the government of India was being remodelled in Parliament,
on its transfer from the Company to the Crown, we
find him praising Mr. Gladstone as the only speaker
of note who had laid stress on the supreme importance
of making 'the Indian nation' contented; and remarking that a time must come when natives will have to
be introduced into the new Council of the Secretary of
State.

In accordance with these principles, Elphinstone
always advocated the importance of maintaining free
intercourse with natives, on the terms of the old

[1] This letter is printed at the end of Cameron's *Address to Parliament on the Duties of Great Britain to India in respect of the Education of the Natives and their Official Employment* (Longmans, 1853).

Marátha simplicity; and he enforced the lesson by his own example. We have already seen how Bishop Heber remarked upon 'the countenance and familiarity which he extends to all the natives of rank who approach him.' So, in his Deccan Report (1819), we find him laying it down that 'gentlemen ought to receive the natives often, when not on business'; for 'this intercourse with the natives is as much a point of duty, and contributes as much to good government, as the details in which we are generally occupied.' And, again, in a letter to Strachey (1821), 'It is not enough to give good laws, or even good courts; you must take the people along with you, and give them a share in your feelings, which can only be done by sharing theirs.' That Elphinstone's own efforts in this direction were not thrown away is attested by the address presented to him on resigning office by the natives of Bombay, in which special stress is laid upon his 'affable and encouraging manners, and freedom from prejudice.'

Elphinstone's interest in education will be remembered as long as the College bearing his name stands at Bombay. But the extent of his interest was by no means limited to the teaching in English now given in that institution. It is hardly too much to say that he was the founder of that system of instruction, both in the vernacular languages and in English, which has contributed as much as its geographical position to give Bombay pre-eminence over certain other provinces. His Minute on Education, dated

March, 1824[1], ranks as an historical document with his Deccan Report; but this is only one of a long series which he wrote on the subject. While at Poona, he had diverted the Dakshina endowment to the foundation of an institution for Sanskrit learning, which has gradually developed into the Poona College; and he took measures to improve the existing village schools by the printing and distribution of well-chosen books of Hindu morality.

At this time, Bombay was probably the most backward of all the Presidencies in respect of education. The chaplains of the Company were expected to supervise a few charity schools, in addition to their other duties. Missionary effort was almost confined to a small party of Americans, who came to Bombay about 1814. A Society for the Promotion of the Education of the Poor, on the model of the Education Society in Bengal, was established in 1820, as the result of a public meeting at which Elphinstone presided; and it was through the voluntary agency of this society that all education in the vernacular languages was conducted during the next sixteen years. Elphinstone obtained for the society a grant of £5000, to be devoted to the printing of books and the purchase of prizes, thus leaving the subscriptions of members free for providing a normal school for training native teachers. He also ordered that an elaborate set of enquiries should be conducted by local officers into

[1] This Minute, but not the others, has been printed by Mr. G. W. Forrest in his *Selections*.

the existing provision for primary instruction. The result of these inquiries, which was not made known until 1832, disclosed a total of 1705 schools with 35,143 scholars in 'the British territories dependent on Bombay,' with a total population estimated at nearly four and three-quarter millions of souls. In the year 1890 the corresponding figures for the whole of Bombay were 11,716 schools and 591,627 pupils; while the population was returned by the Census of 1891 at nearly nineteen millions.

Elphinstone's educational policy encountered no little opposition, from the Court of Directors as well as from his own Council. One of his most cherished projects was to found a college at Bombay for young civilians, on a more modest scale than Wellesley's Fort William College, but with a special department for the training of native officials. The latter part of the scheme was opposed by his colleagues, while the whole failed to obtain the sanction of the authorities at home. He had also great difficulty in preserving the Poona College, though he proved that it was no charge on the Company's revenue, being maintained entirely out of alienated funds. In particular, he defended the professorship of Sanskrit poetry in the following noble plea, inspired by his own enthusiasm for the Greek and Latin classics, for Sanskrit itself was to him a sealed book:

'Even without the example and assistance of a more civilised nation, the science possessed by every people is gradually superseded by their own discoveries as they advance in knowledge, and their early works fall into disuse and into oblivion. But it is otherwise with their poetry: the standard works maintain their reputation undiminished in every age, they form the models of composition and the fountains of classical language; and the writers of the rudest ages are those who contribute the most to the delight and refinement of the most improved of their posterity.'

With regard to the general subject of education, he wrote, in language that has not yet lost its significance:

'It is difficult to imagine an undertaking in which our duty, our interest, and our honour are more immediately concerned. It is now well understood that in all countries the happiness of the poor depends in a great measure on their education. It is by means of it alone that they can acquire those habits of prudence and self-respect from which all other good qualities spring; and if ever there was a country where such habits are required, it is this. We have all often heard of the ills of early marriage and overflowing population; of the savings of a life squandered on some one occasion of festivity; of the helplessness of the *ráyats* which renders them a prey to money-lenders; of their indifference to good clothes and houses, which has been urged on some occasions as an argument against lowering the public demands on them; and finally, of the vanity of all laws to protect them when no individual can be found who has spirit enough to take advantage of those enacted in their favour. There is but one remedy for all this, which is education.'

The actual measures that he proposed are thus summarised:

(1) 'To improve the mode of teaching at the native schools, and to increase their number; (2) to supply them

with school-books; (3) to hold out some encouragement to the lower orders of natives to avail themselves of the means of instruction thus afforded them; (4) to establish schools for teaching the European sciences and improvements in the higher branches of education; (5) to provide for the preparation and publication of books of moral and physical science in native languages; (6) to establish schools for the purpose of teaching English to those disposed to pursue it as a classical language, and as a means of acquiring a knowledge of the European discoveries; (7) to hold forth encouragement to the natives in the pursuit of these last branches of knowledge.'

When judged by the standard to which education in Bombay has long ago attained, this programme may not appear very ambitious; but it was then as much in advance of the spirit of the age as it now is behind it. Elphinstone was himself careful to conciliate the Court of Directors, by arguing that the cost would only to a moderate extent fall upon the Company: that of the schools was to be borne by the villages; that of the prizes and professors by funds already alienated; the press, as the demand for books increased, would be self-supporting; while the services of the vaccinators were to be enlisted as voluntary school-inspectors. At least one member of Council objected to any interference with village schools, arguing that the Government should confine its assistance to English education. No step involving expenditure could be taken without a reference to the authorities at home; and the necessary sanction seems not to have arrived until after Elphinstone had left India. In 1828, the

first English school was opened at Bombay, and about
the same time an English department was attached to
the Sanskrit College at Poona. The battle between
English and the vernacular as the medium of instruction was ultimately fought out at Calcutta, and won
by Macaulay as the champion of English. At Bombay,
the judicious compromise advocated by Elphinstone
long held its ground.

It was fitting that Elphinstone's rule at Bombay
should be commemorated by the establishment of an
English college, towards which natives were the largest
subscribers. When he first heard of the proposal, he
is reported to have said, '*hoc potius mille signis.*'
The original plan was to found 'professorships for the
purpose of teaching the natives the English language,
and the arts, sciences, and literature of Europe—to be
held in the first instance by learned men to be invited
from Great Britain, until natives of the country should
be found perfectly competent to undertake the office.'
A sum of about £27,000 was quickly subscribed, to
which the Government added as much more, and also
allowed a liberal rate of interest on the whole. So
great, however, was the procrastination of those days,
that the Elphinstone Institution was not actually
opened until 1834, seven years after Elphinstone had
left India. It then comprised three objects: (1) a
college department, to which holders of scholarships,
twenty in number, were alone admitted, and where the
subjects taught included English composition, logic,
political economy, higher mathematics, and physical

science; (2) a middle school, in which both English and the vernacular were taught; and (3) a number of vernacular schools. Professorships of botany and chemistry were added in 1846. But it was not until 1873 that the college received its full staff, which now consists of seven professors, of whom all but two are Englishmen. During the last twenty years the principal has been Mr. William Wordsworth, a grandson of the poet. Meanwhile, in 1857, the Elphinstone College found its place within the Bombay University, founded during the year of the Mutiny, while Lord Elphinstone, the nephew of Mountstuart, was Governor of Bombay; and in December, 1868, the new buildings were inaugurated by Lord Mayo, who commented upon the part played by two Elphinstones in the educational history of the Presidency.

We have now accompanied Elphinstone to the close of his Governorship. In those days there was not, as now, a fixed term of five years. But Elphinstone felt that he had ruled long enough. After an unbroken service of more than thirty years, he was fully entitled to claim his retirement. His old longing for home had somewhat died away, but it was succeeded by a strong desire to visit the classical sites of Greece and Italy. He felt that he had done enough for fame, while some accident might imperil the reputation he had won. The dispute with the Supreme Court, and the lack of encouragement in his educational schemes, alike troubled him. Above all, he was doubtful whether his health was not becoming affected by the hot and rainy climate of Bombay. Accordingly, after much deliberation, he finally made up his mind to send in his resignation. This resolve was formed in June, 1826[1], during a farewell visit to the Deccan. By May, 1827, he seems to have received the welcome tidings of Malcolm's appointment as his successor; but he still had to wait until Malcolm arrived in the following October. All through the intervening period his thoughts were elsewhere. He set to work, like a schoolboy, to make a calendar, in which Wednesday (the Council day) was erased week by week for ten months. In February, he wrote in his diary: 'Eight months of India and one of misery at sea are yet to elapse before I stand a single horseman on the desert.' His dreams were all of Greece; and he accumulated a library of Greek travel, beginning with Pausanias, and ending with Clarke and Chandler, Gell and Leake.

Elphinstone handed over office to Malcolm on the 1st of November, 1827, the anniversary of the day on which he had himself taken his seat as Governor eight years before[2]. The following fortnight was occupied with the bitter-sweet festivities of leave-taking, about which his own diary is silent. He was requested to sit to Sir Thomas Lawrence for his portrait, which was placed in the rooms of the

---

[1] Not 1825, as erroneously stated by Colebrooke (ii. 183).

[2] Officially his appointment in England dates from the 7th of October, 1818. See *The Book of Dignities* (ed. 1890), p. 659.

Education Society[1]; and a noble statue by Chantrey also stands in the Town Hall. Addresses poured in upon him—from the British residents in the Presidency, from the civil and military officers serving in the Deccan, from the clergy, and from the members of the Literary Society (the precursor of the Bombay branch of the Asiatic Society). But his best memorial is to be found in the native address announcing the foundation of the Elphinstone Institution, the beginning of which runs as follows:

'We, the native princes, chiefs, gentlemen, and inhabitants of Bombay, its dependencies, and allied territories, cannot contemplate your approaching departure from the country without endeavouring to express, however faintly, the most profound and lasting regret which has been occasioned in our minds by your resignation of the government of this Presidency. For until you became Commissioner in the Deccan and Governor of Bombay, never had we been enabled to appreciate correctly the invaluable benefits which the British dominion is calculated to diffuse throughout the whole of India. But having beheld with admiration, for so long a period, the affable and encouraging manners, the freedom from prejudice, the consideration at all times evinced for the interests and welfare of the people of this country, the regard shown to their ancient customs and laws, the constant endeavours to extend amongst them the inestimable advantages of intellectual and moral improvement, the commanding abilities applied to ensure permanent

[1] This portrait, which is a full-length, now hangs in the Library of Elphinstone College.—Mr. R. G. Oxenham, the present Principal, writes that it was not quite finished when the painter died, and was completed by a pupil.

ameliorations in the condition of all classes, and to promote their prosperity on the soundest principles, by which your private and public conduct has been so pre-eminently distinguished, we are led to consider the influence of the British Government as the most important and desirable blessing which the Supreme Being could have bestowed on our native land.'

May we not say that Oriental hyperbole here coincides with the language of truth?

CHAPTER XI

RETURN HOME: RETIREMENT IN ENGLAND

1828—1859

WHEN Elphinstone left Bombay he was forty-eight years old—an age at which many men in England are only beginning to take a prominent part in public affairs. More than thirty years of life still remained to him; but, though offers of employment were not wanting, his career as a man of action had now finally closed. His health had been affected by thirty-one years' continuous residence in a hot climate; he had acquired a modest competence as the result of his savings; and his personal inclination turned to books, travel, and the society of friends to occupy and soothe the remainder of his days. His early ambition had not been fully satisfied; but as time went on, he distrusted his own abilities, and latterly he shrank, with almost morbid diffidence, from venturing into any untried sphere of activity. More wise than some of his contemporaries, he recognised from the first that his work in India had disqualified him to compete with politicians at home. And his wisdom was still more conspicuously shown by his disinclination to criticise events which had taken place in India under changed circumstances. His unique experience was always at the disposal of those who cared to consult him; but he never volunteered his advice, and he never degenerated into either a partisan or a *laudator temporis acti*. This closing period of his life forms a prolonged evening, golden and mellow, though flecked with clouds, which fitly ends a day of such early promise and sustained achievement.

Elphinstone left Bombay in November, 1827, but he did not arrive in England until May, 1829. The eighteen months that intervened were spent in travelling leisurely through Egypt, Syria, Asia Minor, Greece, and Italy, in company with a doctor and one or two Indian friends. The East happened to be in one of its recurrent paroxysms, which rendered the journey somewhat exciting. The Greek revolt was then at its height, and Russia declared war against Turkey just before the party reached Constantinople. As seems to have been customary before the opening of the overland route, they entered Egypt by way of Kosseir on the Red Sea, the port that had been used by Sir David Baird's Indian expedition some twenty years previously. Thence they marched across the desert to the Nile, where they visited the ruins of Karnak and Thebes, under the guidance of Sir Gardiner Wilkinson. Mehemet Ali was absent from Egypt, but he had left orders that every civility should be extended to them. Their troubles began at Alexandria. They learned that the plague was raging in Palestine, and that they would not be allowed to visit Asia Minor without a firmán from the Porte. At last, they managed to charter a Sardinian vessel, which landed them at Jaffa; and they made a tour through Palestine under the protection of an Austrian passport. This tour was extended as far as Baalbec and the ruined city of Jerash beyond Jordan, then little visited. Returning through the Lebanon, they rejoined their vessel at Beyrout, where they resumed their English nationality, and carried off with them the British consul, in defiance of the Pasha. After touching at Cyprus, and exploring the ruined sites on the seacoast of Lycia, they visited Rhodes and Cos, and finally abandoned their ship at Búdrún, the ancient Halicarnassus. Here they started on their adventurous journey along the mainland to Constantinople, without waiting for a firmán. However, they met everywhere with hospitable entertainment from the Aghas (hereditary chieftains), and reached their destination in safety, *via* Smyrna, Sardis, and the Troad. With an invading army of Russians at Shumla, Constantinople was not a place to linger in, though Elphinstone had no reason to complain of his treatment by the Turks. Accordingly, he engaged a ship for two months, and sailed for Athens.

In the early morning of the 3rd of August (1828) — nearly nine months after leaving Bombay — Elphinstone found himself under the marble columns that crown the cliff of Sunium; and later in the day he was 'electrified with the sight of the Parthenon,' through a telescope. But he was never destined to tread the summit of the Acropolis, the goal of so many years of longing. Athens was then occupied by the Turks, and blockaded by a Greek squadron, whose head-quarters were at Poros, on the opposite shore of the Saronic Gulf. After a delay of ten days, Elphinstone was fortunate enough to obtain the convoy of a British man-of-war, whose captain landed him at the Peiraeus, and gave him letters to the Turkish Selihdár (commandant). No difficulty was now offered to entering Athens, where he stayed for nearly a fortnight, wandering about as if in a dream, his eyes charmed with all he saw, and his mind crowded with classical reminiscences. But neither entreaties nor presents could prevail with the Turks to admit him to the Acropolis, which was then the citadel of the town, and had lately been the scene of fighting. Similar suspicions prevented him from visiting Thermopylae and Delphi. Nevertheless, he wrote of Athens in his diary: 'There is no place I have seen in my travels that I have enjoyed so much, or shall remember with so much pleasure.'

It is interesting to learn what judgment Elphinstone formed of the Turks, after his experience of other Muhammadans:

'Their great fault is their pride, which disgusts one the more because it is religious rather than national. Allowance being made for that, they are very courteous, hospitable, and obliging. They have through all ranks great self-respect, and are far above most of the sorts of meanness practised by other Asiatics. ... They are, however, capricious and obstinate, and apt to be violent, but oftener sullen when opposed. They are ignorant and credulous beyond belief, and will listen to any story that flatters their vanity or falls in with their prejudices. They may seem now to be sensible of the superiority of Europeans in all sorts of knowledge except religious, and most of them seem to see the necessity of some sort of imitation of our system. But none seem prepared for the sacrifice rendered necessary by such a change; and the consequence is almost universal discontent with the present Government, and a total indifference to the success of its measures, foreign or domestic.'

After returning to the Greek head-quarters, Elphinstone visited Eleusis, 'Gell in hand.' At Megara he found Prince Ypsilanti, the Greek generalissimo, who gave him a dinner, at which all had to sit cross-legged. Thence he passed, through Corinth, to Sicyon, Mycenae, Argos, and Tiryns. Concerning the last place, he remarks, in the spirit of Dr. Schliemann:

'It is singular to walk where Hercules has often trod, and to stand on the identical walls from whence he hurled Iphitus.'

At Nauplia, he expresses this opinion of the Greeks, with whom he had not been prepossessed on first acquaintance:

'I find all of that nation very civil, much disposed to acknowledge the assistance of the allies, and by no means such braggarts as I had expected. The country people seem civil quiet men, though not equal to the Turkish peasantry.

They are said to be thieves, to which, from the loss of little articles, I can testify, as well as to their love of music and noise of all kinds. I have not observed them cheat more than other people.'

From Nauplia he went, past the site of Sparta, to the Gulf of Messene, where a French force had just been landed. Here he found Stratford Canning, who had come from Constantinople to confer with Capo d'Istria, who held the title of President of Hellas. But Canning fell to loggerheads with the French and Russian representatives, and some time had yet to pass before the Egyptian troops under Ibrahim Pasha evacuated the Morea. Elphinstone was therefore advised to turn back, instead of going on to Navarino as he had proposed. On his way he paid a very interesting visit to Kolokotroni, the most famous of the Klephts who fought in the War of Independence. At Nauplia he engaged a Greek vessel for a cruise among the Cyclades, and landed at all the islands in turn. Returning once more to the Morea, which was now freed from Turks, he traversed the middle of Arcadia on his way to Olympia, where he commented on the puerility of the Olympic games, and on the comfort of his entertainment in the hovel of a peasant.

Thenceforth he was in a civilised land and among friends; for his cousin, Sir Frederick Adam, was Commissioner of the Ionian Islands, and British cruisers were at his service. One of these landed him at Ithaca, where he was dissatisfied with the identifications of Homeric sites proposed by the inhabitants.

From Corfu he crossed over in a 'steamboat'—which he mentions without surprise or curiosity — to Brindisi. The winter was passed quietly at Naples and Rome, which he frequently revisited in subsequent years; but it may be noted that, on his way to Naples, he turned aside to inspect the battlefield of Cannae. In the spring he directed his steps homewards, through Northern Italy and France. At Venice he had a long conversation with Count Haugwitz, the Prussian Minister; and in Paris he met Talleyrand, at the house of Madame Flahault. He reached Calais on the 1st of May, 1829, and wrote in his diary:

'I close my travels with little hope that I shall ever pass so pleasant a period again. The great charm was the perfect freedom from care and restraint, combined (which it scarce ever is) with perfect exemption from ennui. Whoever wishes to enjoy occupation without labour, and interest without anxiety, or to compress into a moderate period the greatest beauties of art and nature, the most impressive recollections of ancient times, and the most striking peculiarities of modern manners, could scarcely attain his object better than by entering on the journey which I am now concluding.'

Elphinstone returned home, after an absence of thirty-three years, with mingled feelings. The patriotism learnt in the school of Wellesley and Wellington inspired the following reflection at Calais:

'I have long looked on Britain from a distance, not only as my own country, but as the country of great men, and of memorable events; and I feel the same sort of enthusiasm and respect for it that I felt for Italy and Greece.'

And again, when posting up to town through Kent, literary reminiscences overpowered him:

'Every sort of association, from the Edwards and Henrys, Hampden and Sidney, down to Tom Jones and Parson Adams, and almost all the poetical descriptions in our language, combine to heighten the real charms of the rich and beautiful landscape.'

But when once arrived in London, the lonesomeness of the returned exile seized upon him. Long before, at Poona, he had compared Anglo-Indians, looking back to the country where they had been useful and distinguished, to the ghosts of Homer's heroes, who preferred the exertions of a labourer on the earth to all the listless enjoyments of Elysium. So now, he applied to himself the passage in the Odyssey (ii. 174), where Halitherses prophesies concerning Ulysses:

Φῆν κακὰ πολλὰ παθόντ', ὀλέσαντ' ἄπο πάντας ἑταίρους,
'Αγνωστον πάντεσσι [τριακοστῷ] ἐνιαυτῷ
Οἴκαδ' ἐλεύσεσθαι.

It may be doubted whether Elphinstone ever became completely naturalised to English life. He had few strong ties remaining, either of blood or friendship. The publicity and garrulousness of politics were alike abhorrent to him; nor would his pride allow him to take part in those semi-public duties that are expected from a country gentleman. His constitutional shyness grew upon him, and he gradually retired more and more into the seclusion of his own library. After a few trips to Scotland, to revisit his boyish haunts, and to exercise his privilege as a county elector, and several winters passed in Italy, he settled down as an old man before his time—first, in chambers in the Albany, and afterwards at Hookwood, a retired country-house in Surrey, near the borders of Kent. Not that he became a recluse until the very last. On his first arrival in England he mixed freely in society. He was elected a member of 'The Club' and of the Dilettanti; he subscribed to Almack's, and he frequented the theatre and the opera. He was a welcome guest at Holland House; and while at Edinburgh made the acquaintance of Cockburn and Jeffrey and Sir Walter Scott. Even after his health had failed, he was always glad to receive visitors who were connected with India, or who could converse with him on literary subjects.

When the whole course of his life in England is considered, there can be little doubt of the correctness of his own decision, that his public career was finished. But it was natural that his friends should think differently. During his first season in London (1829), Anglo-Indians talked about him as destined to be employed at the head of the Board of Control. His relatives urged him to enter Parliament as member for Lanarkshire, where his family still exercised influence. The Duke of Wellington, who was now Premier, openly said that he ought to return to India, possibly as Governor-General. Lord Ellenborough, doubtless at the Duke's suggestion, offered him the post of Ambassador to Persia; but Elphinstone replied that 'nothing would ever induce him to go to Asia again.' A few years later, after the novelty of his freedom had worn off, he was more strongly tempted. In August, 1834, when Lord William Bentinck's term of office as Governor-General was drawing to a close, the Chairman of the Company wrote to him, proposing to submit his name to the Ministry, together with that of Metcalfe, as Lord William's successor. Elphinstone pleaded physical infirmity, in the words of Evander (Virg. *Aen.* viii. 508, 509):

> 'Sed mihi tarda gelu morbisque[1] effeta senectus
> Invidet imperium.'

Nor could he be moved from his determination by a second more pressing letter. Towards the end of this year, the Whig Ministry was dismissed, and Lord Ellenborough came back to the Board of Control. One of his first acts was to endeavour to secure Elphinstone's services as permanent Under-Secretary. When this failed, he offered Elphinstone the still vacant succession to the Governor-Generalship; but again in vain. A few weeks later, Elphinstone received yet another proposal—to proceed to Canada as Commissioner to settle the bitter quarrel then raging between the colony and the mother-country. When he refused this also, Metcalfe, already stricken with a mortal illness, undertook the duty.

It is not altogether easy to appreciate Elphinstone's

---

[1] *saeclisque* in the original.

motives for declining the Governor-Generalship, though they have been printed at length by his biographer. He was only fifty-five years old, and had still, as it turned out, twenty-five years more before him; while Cornwallis went out for the second time to India at the age of sixty-six. And his refusal stands out more prominently in the light of history, when one reflects that he might have saved India from the First Afghan War. Elphinstone himself wrote in his diary, with a reminiscence of Walter Scott:

'If there had been the least prospect of usefulness or distinction, I should not have thought of my health for a single moment. I am much cooled since old times, but I would still give all the rest of my life with delight for one moment of real glory.'

The truth seems to be, he was firmly persuaded that the situation in India was not such as to demand from him the sacrifice of his literary leisure; while he was equally convinced that the ordinary duties of the office would be distasteful to him, and that his health would certainly break down. Accordingly, he permitted his personal inclinations to bias his sense of duty; and for this error of judgment he must be condemned to occupy a lower place than he might otherwise have held among the Rulers of India.

A few years later, his health did break down. In March, 1836, he was compelled to withdraw from the Royal Commission appointed to inquire into the means of religious instruction in Scotland, on which he had accepted a seat. In the autumn of 1839, he suffered from another sharp attack of illness, a recurrence of which, in the winter of 1840-41, left him ever afterwards an invalid.

But before this he had managed to write and publish his *History of India*, by which his name is perhaps best known at this day to the general public. The design of such an enterprise had long occupied his mind, ever since his literary ambition was first stirred by the favourable reception of his work on Kábul. So far back as 1816, while he was still Resident at the court of the Peshwa, we find the following entries in his diary:

'It struck me this morning, in talking after breakfast about the revolutions in Poona, that an interesting history might be produced of the Marátha empire, and that the time when such a work might be produced is rapidly passing away.'

And a few months later:

'It has always been a great source of uneasiness to me that I should be at a loss for something to do after I go to England. To remedy this, I have thought of writing a Marátha history, or a history of the fall of the Mughal empire and the rise of ours. I now think of a translation of Arrian, with a commentary, chiefly geographical.'

Ten years afterwards, while at Bombay, the same idea recurs, as a solace for old age:

'This may be obtained if one can enter on any long work that holds out a reasonable prospect of reputation: such, for instance, as a history of India. But this must not be undertaken too soon.'

Elphinstone does not seem to have made any special

collections for the purpose while in India, though Hindu antiquities and Muhammadan chronicles always interested him; nor do we find him complaining of the loss of his library, burnt just before the battle of Kirkí. The history of the Maráthás he resigned in favour of his friend and former assistant, Captain Grant Duff, whom he assisted with references to public and private documents, and whose early chapters he subjected to a critical but sympathetic revision. Another friend, Erskine, took up the history of the early Mughals, though his learned works failed to meet with popular favour.

It was not until 1834, when he had been five years at home, that Elphinstone seriously addressed himself to his task, at the very time that he was refusing the Governor-Generalship. His first draft of the early Hindu period was finished in a few months, and then laid aside. In 1836, he again took up the work, and went steadily on with it. After completing his sketch of the Muhammadan period, he began to write the story of the foundation of British rule, which had always formed part of his original design. But many circumstances now conspired to damp the enterprise. His health was perceptibly failing, each successive attack of illness leaving him more feeble. He distrusted his own capacity for continuous narrative. An examination of Mill's standard History showed him that his own estimate of persons and events did not materially differ from the accepted one. Finally, the appearance of Macaulay's two famous essays on

Clive (January, 1840) and Warren Hastings (October, 1841) confirmed him in his resolution to abandon the English period of Indian history.

Meanwhile, he had consulted Jeffrey about the advisability of bringing out the earlier portion by itself. Jeffrey's advice to publish was warm and decided, though it was not accompanied by any extravagant estimate of the book. John Murray undertook the publication; and in 1841 appeared *The History of India — Hindu and Mahometan Periods*, which shows, by its title-page, that it was intended to be introductory to a larger work. Such as it is, it has held its own to the present day, with the notes of Prof. E. B. Cowell, as the standard authority on the period. If it be found dull by the general reader, that may fairly be set down to the subject; the knowledge, the clearness, the impartiality, the sympathetic treatment, are Elphinstone's own. In 1887, Sir T. E. Colebrooke put together out of Elphinstone's papers a posthumous volume, to which he gave the title of *The Rise of the British Power in the East*. This only covers the epoch of Clive; and, while the sketch of Clive's character was worth preserving, it must be confessed that a perusal of the book justifies the author's self-criticism, that he had no talent for narration.

Though Elphinstone lived for eighteen years after the publication of his *History*, little more remains to be said. He had become a confirmed invalid. Drowsiness, deafness, weakness of sight, and other physical infirmities anticipated the approach of old age.

But his intellectual faculties remained unimpaired to the last; and with them survived his interests in India and in literature. Indian governors, young Members of Parliament, and political writers alike came to consult the Sage of Hookwood on Oriental affairs. He took an active interest in the debate in the House of Commons on the bill for transferring the government from the Company to the Crown, only a year before his death.

'He was always a great reader of novels, and during the first year or two of his country life he gave himself up to the drama, ancient and modern. One of the volumes of journals, ranging over about a year, consists almost solely of short notes on the plays of Ben Jonson, Marlowe, Beaumont and Fletcher, Shirley, Massinger, Congreve and Otway, Plautus and Terence, Metastasio, Monti, and Molière, with occasional glimpses of Shakspere and Euripides.

'His love for poetry amounted to a passion. He would discuss his favourite authors with the enthusiasm of a boy; and one of the last occasions on which he left home on any tour of pleasure was to visit, in Cornwall, the scenes of King Arthur's battles.'

In view of the practice of the present day, it may appear strange that Elphinstone never received any mark of titular distinction. After the battle of Kirkí, indeed, he was offered a baronetcy, which his family declined on his behalf, and he entirely acquiesced in their decision. At that time, it seems that he would have been pleased with the Commandership of the Bath in the civil division, with which Malcolm's services were rewarded. He was never admitted to the Privy

Council, as was Holt Mackenzie, on being appointed to the Board of Control. His biographer does not confirm the rumour, which has found its way into print, that he refused the peerage which Metcalfe accepted. Oxford alone recognised his merits by conferring upon him the honorary degree of D.C.L. at the Commemoration of 1834.

No record of Mountstuart Elphinstone would be complete which omitted all mention of his religious views. Bishop Heber[1], in defending him against an absurd imputation of being 'devoid of religion and blinded to all spiritual truth,' erred somewhat in the other direction, by ascribing to him greater orthodoxy than he ever professed. The truth is, that in his younger days he had passed through a phase of scepticism characteristic of the time; but that experience of the world and much reading converted him to what may be termed a devout Unitarian. His outward rule of life was based upon the maxims of the Stoic philosophy. Among modern divines, he studied most, and recommended chiefly to others, Butler, Paley, and Lardner. In the Bible, he preferred the Sermon on the Mount to all else. Of Pope's Universal Prayer, he said: 'It is almost the first prayer I ever learned, and the one I should wish last to utter. Every word it contains is what I could say from the heart.'

Death came to Elphinstone suddenly, without mental decay and without pain. On the night of the 20th of

---

[1] *Narrative of a Journey*, &c. (vol. ii, p. 221).

November, 1859, he was seized by paralysis, and passed away in a few hours. He had just entered his eighty-first year. He was buried in the churchyard of Limpsfield, adjoining the grounds of Hookwood, where Lord Elphinstone, his nephew and successor in the government of Bombay, desired that his own remains also should be laid. In the following February, a meeting of his friends and admirers was held in Willis's Rooms, to take steps for preserving his memory. It was resolved to place a statue of him by Noble in St. Paul's. Of the memorials at Bombay mention has already been made. There is also a full-length portrait at the Oriental Club, painted by Pickersgill, an admirable engraving of which in vignette [1] forms the frontispiece to the second volume of Colebrooke's biography.

Elphinstone's statue in St. Paul's stands in the north aisle, facing that of Sir Pulteney Malcolm, the brother of his friend. Beneath is inscribed the simple epitaph :

MEMBER OF THE INDIAN CIVIL SERVICE

GOVERNOR OF BOMBAY

AND HISTORIAN OF EARLY INDIA.

---

[1] The original plate of this engraving has been lent by Mr. John Murray to illustrate the present volume.

INDEX

ADAM, Sir Frederick, 206.
ADAM, John, 10, 19, 39, 75, 161.
ADÁLAT (Civil Court), 122, 131, 133, 152, 167, 173.
AMÍR KHÁN, 64, 119.
ANTIQUARIAN INTERESTS, 73, 84, 90, 204-207, 209, 212.
ARAB MERCENARIES, 39, 116.
ARGÁUM, battle of, 39, 40.
ASHTÍ, battle of, 117.
ASSAYE, battle of, 36-38.
ATHENS, visit to, 204.

BÁJÍ RÁO, see Peshwa.
BARLOW, Sir George, 47, 85.
BASSEIN, treaty of, 32, 33, 37.
BENARES, massacre of, 21.
BENTHAM, Jeremy, 124, 147, 153, 156, 179, 180.
BHARTPUR, repulse of Lake at, 34, 48.
BHARTPUR, capture of, by Combermere, 160.
BHONSLA, see Nágpur, Rájá of.
BRIGGS, Captain, 95, 98, 126.
BURR, Colonel, 109, 111.

CAMERON, Charles Hay, 190.
CANADA, 210.
CANNING, George (quoted), 112-115.
CANNING, Stratford, 206.
CHAPLIN, Mr., 127, 141, 152, 160, 172.
CHERRY, Mr., massacre of, 21.

CHANTREY, statue by, 198.
CHINA, compared with India, 82, 185, 187, 188.
CLOSE, Barry, 10, 29, 32, 34, 35, 52.
COLEBROOKE, Sir T. E. (quoted), 17, 136, 178, 214.
CODIFICATION OF LAW, 179-184.
CUTCH, settlement of, 169.

DAVIS, SAMUEL, 20, 21, 23.
DECCAN, settlement of, 121-158.

EDUCATIONAL REFORMS, 147, 188-190, 191-197.
EGYPT, visit to, 202.
ELLENBOROUGH, Lord, 209, 210.
ELLIOT, Sir Walter, 173.
ELPHINSTONE, James, 20.
ELPHINSTONE, Lord, 197, 217.
ELPHINSTONE, Mountstuart: Summary of life, 10, 11 : birth and family, 17, 18 : arrival in India, 19 : massacre of Benares, 20, 21 : at College of Fort William, 22 : first appointment to Poona, 23; journey through Orissa, 24 : Madras and Mysore, 25 : at Haidarábád, 26 : books read during the year, 27, 28 : with Close at Poona, 29 : secretary to General Wellesley, 35 : capture of Ahmadnagar, 35 ; battle of Assaye, 36-38 : camp-life, 38 : battle of Argáum, 39, 40 :

storm of Gáwalgarh, 41-43:
Resident at Nágpur, 45-54:
visit to Calcutta, 52, 53: Resident with Sindia, 54-58: description of Sindia's camp, 55,
56: the Kábul mission, 58-74:
official report of mission, 74:
resident at Poona, 75-120:
settlement of Jagírdárs, 77-80:
book on Kábul, 80-82: character of the Peshwa, 87, 88:
murder of the Shástri, 89, 90:
surrender and escape of Trimbakjí, 90-92: revolt of Trimbakjí, 94-100: battle of Kirkí,
106-113: eulogy by Canning,
112, 113: conquest of the Deccan, 114-119: battle of Koregáon, 116: settlement of the
Deccan, 121-158: restoration
of Rájá of Sátára, 121-123:
settlement of the Jagírdárs,
130-133: treatment of the
Bráhmans, 134, 135: fiscal reforms, 136-139: police, 139-
141: criminal justice, 142-147:
civil justice and *panchâyats*,
148-155: governor of Bombay,
159-200: character by Heber,
163-165: foreign affairs, 165:
visits to Gujarát, 165-167: the
Gáekwár of Baroda, 168: the
Ráo of Cutch, 169: the peninsula of Káthiáwár, 170: the
Máhí Kántha, 171: the outbreak at Kittúr, 172-173: the
Supreme Court, 173-178: deportation of an editor, 174-176:
codification of the law, 179-184:
admission of natives to office,
184-191: promotion of education, 191-197: native address
on retirement, 199: return
home, 201-203: in Egypt, 202:
in Palestine, through Asia
Minor, at Constantinople, 203:
tour in Greece, 203-206: winter
in Italy, 207: arrival in England, 208: retired life at home,
208-217: refusal of Governor-Generalship, 210, 211: History
of India, 212-214: failure of
health, and old age, 214, 215:
religious views, 216: death and
burial, 216, 217: monument in
St. Paul's, 217.

ELPHINSTONE COLLEGE, 196, 197,
199.

ENGLISH LITERATURE, study of,
15, 28, 52, 82, 164, 215, 216.

ERSKINE, William, 76, 80, 84,
124, 156, 179, 180, 185, 213.

FORREST, G. W. (quoted), 96, 125,
129.

FRENCH, in India, 12, 26, 33, 39,
60.

FRENCH, study of, 28, 82, 164, 215.

GÁEKWÁR, the (of Baroda), 86,
89-91, 168, 169.

GÁWALGARH, storm of, 41-43.

GLADSTONE, Mr., 190.

GOA, 76, 157.

GOVERNOR-GENERALSHIP, refused,
210, 211.

GRANT DUFF, Captain, 108, 123,
213.

GREECE, archaeological tour in,
92, 197, 198, 202-206.

GREEK, study of, 19, 20, 27, 30,
52, 82, 93, 164, 198, 215.

GREEK quotations, 43, 47, 158,
208.

GÚRKHA WAR, 86.

GUJARÁT, visits to, 165-172.

HASTINGS, Marquis of, 85, 86,
101, 117, 121.

HEBER, Bishop, 100: his character
of Elphinstone, 163-165, 168,
176, 216.

HISLOP, Sir Thomas, 101-103.

HOG-HUNTING, 13, 79, 93, 163.

HOLKAR, 32, 33, 34, 48, 57, 86,
101, 104, 119.

ITALIAN, study of, 28, 82, 164,
215.

ITALY, visits to, 207, 209.

INDEX

JÁGÍRDÁRS, settlement of, 78-80, 130-133.
JEFFREY, Lord, 209, 214.
JEFFREYS, Dr., 82, 93.
JENKINS, Mr., 10, 51, 52, 56, 80, 118.

KÁRLÍ, caves at, 84.
KÁBUL, mission to, 59-74.
KÁBUL, account of, 80-82.
KÁTHIÁWÁR, settlement of, 168, 170.
KEITH, Lord, 18, 20.
KIRKÍ, battle of, 12, 110-113.
KIRKPATRICK, Colonel, 22.
KIRKPATRICK, Major, 26, 27.
KOLHÁPUR, 78. 172.
KOREGÁON, battle of, 116.

LAKE, Lord, 33, 34, 39, 48, 124.
LATIN, study of, 27, 28, 37, 38, 52, 65, 84, 87, 93, 164, 207, 210.
LAW REFORMS, 145-155, 178-184.
LAWRENCE, Sir T., portrait by, 198.

MACAULAY, Lord, referred to, 15, 196, 213.
MACKINTOSH, Sir James, 52, 76, 80, 81, 173, 185.
MALCOLM, Sir John, 11-13, 15, 16, 34, 35, 43, 76, 80, 81, 101-105, 115, 119, 128, 133, 159, 162, 185, 198, 216.
MÁHI KÁNTHA, settlement of, 168, 171.
MARÁTHÁS, the, 29, 48, 49, 55, 57, 83, 85, 87-89.
MARTYN, Henry, 76.
MEHIDPUR, battle of, 13, 119.
METCALFE, Lord, 11, 12, 14, 15, 16, 58, 61, 176, 186, 210, 216.
MINTO, Lord, 47, 53, 59-61, 78.
MONSON, Colonel, 34, 48.
MUNRO, Sir Thomas, 11, 12, 13, 14, 16, 114, 127, 159, 187.
MYSORE, 25, 33, 39.

NÁGPUR, Rájá of, 31-34, 39, 41, 43, 47, 48-49, 86, 101, 118, 119.
NAPOLEON, dread of, 12, 31, 60, 69.
NOBLE, statue by, 217.

ORISSA, journey through, 24; conquest of, 33, 98.

PALESTINE, visit to, 203.
PANCHÁYATS, 148-155.
PERSIA, mission to, 60.
PERSIAN, study of, 20, 27, 50, 164.
PERSIAN GULF, disturbances in, 165.
PESHÁWAR, 65-72.
PESHWA (Bájí Ráo), character of, 87, 88.
PICKERSGILL, portrait by, 217.
PINDÁRÍS, 36, 49-51, 85, 86, 101, 119.
POONA, 22, 29, 33, 34.
PRESS, freedom of, 174-176.
PUBLIC SPEAKING, abhorrence of, 161.

RANJÍT, SINGH, mission of Metcalfe to, 61.
RELIGIOUS VIEWS, 216.
RUSSIA, dread of, 185.

SANSKRIT COLLEGE at Poona, 135, 193, 196.
SÁTÁRA, Rájá of, 78, 117, 118, 121-123.
SCOTT, Sir Walter, 52, 82, 209, 211.
SHÁH SHÚJA, description of, 66, 72.
SHÁSTRI, Gangádhar, murder of, 89, 90.
SIND, 165.
SINDIA, 31-34, 39, 41, 43, 47, 48, 54-57, 86, 104, 105, 118, 119.
SÍTABALDÍ, battle of, 118, 119.
SMITH, General Lionel, 99, 104, 105, 110, 113-117.
STEPHEN, Sir James (quoted), 180.
STEVENSON, General, 33, 36, 38, 40, 41.

STRACHEY, Edward, 20, 22–26, 35, 39, 75, 92, 122, 174, 179.
SUPREME COURT, 173–178.
SURJI ANJANGÁON, treaty of, 43.

TEIGNMOUTH, Lord, 20.
TRIMBAKJÍ, 88–92, 94–97, 99, 100.

WEBBE, Josiah, 10, 45.
WELLESLEY, Arthur (Duke of Wellington), 14, 26, 31, 33–47, 77, 209.
WELLESLEY, Marquis, 10, 22, 31–34, 44, 47, 53.

ZEMÁN SHÁH, 20, 62, 73.

THE END.

RULERS OF INDIA:

THE CLARENDON PRESS SERIES OF INDIAN HISTORICAL RETROSPECTS.

Edited by SIR W. W. HUNTER, K.C.S.I., M.A., LL.D.

The following 26 volumes have been published :—

I. *A BRIEF HISTORY OF THE INDIAN PEOPLES*, by SIR WILLIAM WILSON HUNTER, K.C.S.I. Twenty-first Edition; 82nd thousand. Price 3s. 6d.

II. *AKBAR: and the Rise of the Mughal Empire*, by COLONEL MALLESON, C.S.I., Author of *A History of the Indian Mutiny; The History of Afghanistan*. Fourth thousand. 2s. 6d.

III. *ALBUQUERQUE: and the Early Portuguese Settlements in India*, by H. MORSE STEPHENS, Esq., M.A., Balliol College, Lecturer on Indian History at Cambridge, Author of *The French Revolution; The Story of Portugal, &c.* 2s. 6d.

IV. *AURANGZÍB: and the Decay of the Mughal Empire*, by STANLEY LANE POOLE, Esq., B.A., Author of *The Coins of the Mughal Emperors; The Life of Stratford Canning; Catalogue of Indian Coins in the British Museum, &c.* 2s. 6d.

V. *MADHAVA RAO SINDHIA: and the Hindú Reconquest of India*, by H. G. KEENE, Esq., M.A., C.I.E., Author of *The Moghul Empire, &c.* 2s. 6d.

VI. *LORD CLIVE: and the Establishment of the English in India*, by COLONEL MALLESON, C.S.I. 2s. 6d.

VII. *DUPLEIX: and the Struggle for India by the European Nations*, by COLONEL MALLESON, C.S.I., Author of *The History of the French in India, &c.* Fourth thousand. 2s. 6d.

VIII. *WARREN HASTINGS: and the Founding of the British Administration*, by CAPTAIN L. J. TROTTER, Author of *India under Victoria, &c.* Fourth thousand. 2s. 6d.

IX. *THE MARQUESS CORNWALLIS: and the Consolidation of British Rule*, by W. S. SETON-KARR, Esq., sometime Foreign Secretary to the Government of India, Author of *Selections from the Calcutta Gazettes*, 3 vols. (1784-1805). Third thousand. 2s. 6d.

X. *HAIDAR ALÍ AND TIPÚ SULTÁN: and the Struggle with the Muhammadan Powers of the South*, by LEWIN BENTHAM BOWRING, Esq., C.S.I., sometime Private Secretary to the Viceroy (Lord Canning) and Chief Commissioner of Mysore, Author of *Eastern Experiences.* 2s. 6d.

XI. *THE MARQUESS WELLESLEY: and the Development of the Company into the Supreme Power in India*, by the Rev. W. H. HUTTON, M.A., Fellow and Tutor of St. John's College, Oxford. 2s. 6d.

XII. *THE MARQUESS OF HASTINGS: and the Final Overthrow of the Maráthá Power*, by MAJOR ROSS OF BLADENSBURG, C.B., Coldstream Guards; F.R.G.S. 2s. 6d.

RULERS OF INDIA SERIES (*continued*).

XIII. *MOUNTSTUART ELPHINSTONE: and the Making of South-Western India*, by J. S. COTTON, Esq., M.A., formerly Fellow of Queen's College, Oxford, Author of *The Decennial Statement of the Moral and Material Progress and Condition of India*, presented to Parliament (1885), &c. 2s. 6d.

XIV. *SIR THOMAS MUNRO: and the British Settlement of the Madras Presidency*, by JOHN BRADSHAW, Esq., M.A., LL.D., Inspector of Schools, Madras. 2s. 6d.

XV. *EARL AMHERST: and the British Advance eastwards to Burma*, chiefly from unpublished papers of the Amherst family, by Mrs. ANNE THACKERAY RITCHIE, Author of *Old Kensington, &c.*, and RICHARDSON EVANS, Esq. 2s. 6d.

XVI. *LORD WILLIAM BENTINCK: and the Company as a Governing and Non-trading Power*, by DEMETRIUS BOULGER, Esq., Author of *England and Russia in Central Asia; The History of China, &c.* 2s. 6d.

XVII. *EARL OF AUCKLAND: and the First Afghan War*, by CAPTN. L. J. TROTTER, Author of *India under Victoria*. 2s. 6d.

XVIII. *VISCOUNT HARDINGE: and the Advance of the British Dominions into the Punjab*, by his Son and Private Secretary, the Right Hon. VISCOUNT HARDINGE. Third thousand. 2s. 6d.

XIX. *RANJIT SINGH: and the Sikh Barrier between our Growing Empire and Central Asia*, by SIR LEPEL GRIFFIN, K.C.S.I., Author of *The Punjab Chiefs, &c.* Third thousand. 2s. 6d.

XX. *JOHN RUSSELL COLVIN: the last Lieutenant-Governor of the North-Western Provinces under the Company*, by his son, SIR AUCKLAND COLVIN, K.C.S.I., late Lieutenant-Governor of the North-Western Provinces. 2s. 6d.

XXI. *THE MARQUESS OF DALHOUSIE: and the Final Development of the Company's Rule*, by SIR WILLIAM WILSON HUNTER, K.C.S.I., M.A. Seventh thousand. 2s. 6d.

XXII. *CLYDE AND STRATHNAIRN: and the Suppression of the Great Revolt*, by MAJOR-GENERAL SIR OWEN TUDOR BURNE, K.C.S.I., sometime Military Secretary to the Commander-in-Chief in India. Fourth thousand. 2s. 6d.

XXIII. *EARL CANNING: and the Transfer of India from the Company to the Crown*, by SIR HENRY S. CUNNINGHAM, K.C.I.E., M.A., Author of *British India and its Rulers, &c.* Third thousand. 2s. 6d.

XXIV. *LORD LAWRENCE: and the Reconstruction of India under the Crown*, by SIR CHARLES UMPHERSTON AITCHISON, K.C.S.I., LL.D., formerly Foreign Secretary to the Government of India, and Lieutenant-Governor of the Punjab. Third thousand. 2s. 6d.

XXV. *THE EARL OF MAYO: and the Consolidation of the Queen's Rule in India*, by SIR WILLIAM WILSON HUNTER, K.C.S.I., M.A., LL.D. Third thousand. 2s. 6d.

SUPPLEMENTARY VOLUME.

XXVI. *JAMES THOMASON: and the British Settlement of North-Western India*, by SIR RICHARD TEMPLE, Bart., M.P., formerly Lieutenant-Governor of Bengal, and Governor of Bombay. Price 3s. 6d.

The Clarendon Press History of India, 3s. 6d.

A BRIEF HISTORY OF THE INDIAN PEOPLES.

STANDARD EDITION (TWENTY-FIRST), REVISED TO 1895.
EIGHTY-SECOND THOUSAND.

This Edition incorporates the suggestions received by the author from Directors of Public Instruction and other educational authorities in India; its statistics are brought down to the Census of 1891; and its narrative to 1892. The work has received the emphatic approval of the organ of the English School Boards, and has been translated into five languages. It is largely employed for educational purposes in Europe and America and as a text-book prescribed by the University of Calcutta for its Entrance Examination from 1886 to 1891.

'"A Brief History of the Indian Peoples," by W. W. Hunter, presents a sort of bird's-eye view both of India and of its people from the earliest dawn of historical records . . . . A work of authority and of original value.'—*The Daily News* (London).

'Dr. Hunter may be said to have presented a compact epitome of the results of his researches into the early history of India; a subject upon which his knowledge is at once exceptionally wide and exceedingly thorough.'—*The Scotsman.*

'Within the compass of some 250 pages we know of no history of the people of India so concise, so interesting, and so useful for educational purposes as this.'—*The School Board Chronicle* (London).

'For its size and subject there is not a better written or more trustworthy history in existence.'—*The Journal of Education.*

'So thoroughly revised as to entitle it to separate notice.'—*The Times.*

'Dr. Hunter's history, if brief, is comprehensive. It is a storehouse of facts marshalled in a masterly style; and presented, as history should be, without the slightest suspicion of prejudice or suggestion of partisanship. Dr. Hunter observes a style of severe simplicity, which is the secret of an impressive presentation of details.'—*The Daily Review* (Edinburgh).

'By far the best manual of Indian History that has hitherto been published, and quite equal to any of the Historical Series for Schools edited by Dr. Freeman. We trust that it will soon be read in all the schools in this Presidency.'—*The Times of India.*

Extract from a criticism by Edward Giles, Esq., Inspector of Schools, Northern Division, Bombay Presidency:—'What we require is a book which shall be accurate as to facts, but not overloaded with them; written in a style which shall interest, attract, and guide uncultivated readers; and short, because it must be sold at a reasonable price. These conditions have never, in my opinion, been realized previous to the introduction of this book.'

'The publication of the Hon. W. W. Hunter's "School History of India" is an event in literary history.'—*Reis & Rayyet* (Calcutta).

'He has succeeded in writing a history of India, not only in such a way that it will be read, but also in a way which we hope will lead young Englishmen and young natives of India to think more kindly of each other. The Calcutta University has done wisely in prescribing this brief history as a text-book for the Entrance Examination.'—*The Hindoo Patriot* (Calcutta).

P

Opinions of the Press
ON
SIR WILLIAM HUNTER'S 'DALHOUSIE.'

'An interesting and exceedingly readable volume. . . . Sir William Hunter has produced a valuable work about an important epoch in English history in India, and he has given us a pleasing insight into the character of a remarkable Englishman. The "Rulers of India" series, which he has initiated, thus makes a successful beginning in his hands with one who ranks among the greatest of the great names which will be associated with the subject.'—*The Times.*

'To no one is the credit for the improved condition of public intelligence [regarding India] more due than to Sir William Hunter. From the beginning of his career as an Indian Civilian he has devoted a rare literary faculty to the task of enlightening his countrymen on the subject of England's greatest dependency. . . . By inspiring a small army of fellow-labourers with his own spirit, by inducing them to conform to his own method, and shaping a huge agglomeration of facts into a lucid and intelligible system, Sir W. Hunter has brought India and its innumerable interests within the pale of achievable knowledge, and has given definite shape to the truths which its history establishes and the problems which it suggests. . . . Such contributions to literature are apt to be taken as a matter of course, because their highest merit is to conceal the labour, and skill, and knowledge involved in their production; but they raise the whole level of public intelligence, and generate an atmosphere in which the baleful influences of folly, ignorance, prejudice, and presumption dwindle and disappear.'—*Saturday Review.*

'Admirably calculated to impart in a concise and agreeable form a clear general outline of the history of our great Indian Empire.'—*Economist.*

'A skilful and most attractive picture. . . . The author has made good use of public and private documents, and has enjoyed the privilege of being aided by the deceased statesman's family. His little work is, consequently, a valuable contribution to modern history.'—*Academy.*

'The book should command a wide circle of readers, not only for its author's sake and that of its subject, but partly at least on account of the very attractive way in which it has been published at the moderate price of half-a-crown. But it is, of course, by its intrinsic merits alone that a work of this nature should be judged. And those merits are everywhere conspicuous. . . . A writer whose thorough mastery of all Indian subjects has been acquired by years of practical experience and patient research.'—*The Athenæum.*

'Never have we been so much impressed by the great literary abilities of Sir William Hunter as we have been by the perusal of "The Marquess of Dalhousie." . . . The knowledge displayed by the writer of the motives of Lord Dalhousie's action, of the inner working of his mind, is so complete, that Lord Dalhousie himself, were he living, could not state them more clearly. . . . Sir William Hunter's style is so clear, his language so vivid, and yet so simple, conveying the impressions he wishes so perspicuously that they cannot but be understood, that the work must have a place in every library, in every home, we might say indeed every cottage.'—*Evening News.*

'Sir William Hunter has written an admirable little volume on "The Marquess of Dalhousie" for his series of the "Rulers of India." It can be read at a sitting, yet its references—expressed or implied—suggest the study and observation of half a life-time.'—*The Daily News.*

Opinions of the Press
ON
SIR WILLIAM HUNTER'S 'LORD MAYO.'

'Sir William W. Hunter has contributed a brief but admirable biography of the Earl of Mayo to the series entitled "Rulers of India," edited by himself (Oxford, at the Clarendon Press).'—*The Times.*

'In telling this story in the monograph before us, Sir William Hunter has combined his well-known literary skill with an earnest sympathy and fulness of knowledge which are worthy of all commendation.... The world is indebted to the author for a fit and attractive record of what was eminently a noble life.'—*The Academy.*

'The sketch of The Man is full of interest, drawn as it is with complete sympathy, understanding, and appreciation. But more valuable is the account of his administration. No one can show so well and clearly as Sir William Hunter does what the policy of Lord Mayo contributed to the making of the Indian Empire of to-day.'—*The Scotsman.*

'Sir William Hunter has given us a monograph in which there is a happy combination of the essay and the biography. We are presented with the main features of Lord Mayo's administration unencumbered with tedious details which would interest none but the most official of Anglo-Indians; while in the biography the man is brought before us, not analytically, but in a life-like portrait.'—*Vanity Fair.*

'The story of his life Sir W. W. Hunter tells in well-chosen language —clear, succinct, and manly. Sir W. W. Hunter is in sympathy with his subject, and does full justice to Mayo's strong, genuine nature. Without exaggeration and in a direct, unaffected style, as befits his theme, he brings the man and his work vividly before us.'—*The Glasgow Herald.*

'All the knowledge acquired by personal association, familiarity with administrative details of the Indian Government, and a strong grasp of the vast problems to be dealt with, is utilised in this presentation of Lord Mayo's personality and career. Sir W. Hunter, however, never overloads his pages, and the outlines of the sketch are clear and firm.' —*The Manchester Express.*

'This is another of the "Rulers of India" series, and it will be hard to beat.... Sir William Hunter's perception and expression are here at their very best.'—*The Pall Mall Gazette.*

'The latest addition to the "Rulers of India" series yields to none of its predecessors in attractiveness, vigour, and artistic portraiture.... The final chapter must either be copied verbally and literally—which the space at our disposal will not permit—or be left to the sorrowful perusal of the reader. The man is not to be envied who can read it with dry eyes.'—*Allen's Indian Mail.*

'The little volume which has just been brought out is a study of Lord Mayo's career by one who knew all about it and was in full sympathy with it.... Some of these chapters are full of spirit and fire. The closing passages, the picture of the Viceroy's assassination, cannot fail to make any reader hold his breath. We know what is going to happen, but we are thrilled as if we did not know it, and were still held in suspense. The event itself was so terribly tragic that any ordinary description might seem feeble and laggard. But in this volume we are made to feel as we must have felt if we had been on the spot and seen the murderer "fastened like a tiger" on the back of the Viceroy.'—*Daily News*, Leading Article.

Opinions of the Press

ON

MR. W. S. SETON-KARR'S 'CORNWALLIS.'

'This new volume of the "Rulers of India" series keeps up to the high standard set by the author of "The Marquess of Dalhousie." For dealing with the salient passages in Lord Cornwallis's Indian career no one could have been better qualified than the whilom foreign secretary to Lord Lawrence.'—*The Athenæum.*

'We hope that the volumes on the "Rulers of India" which are being published by the Clarendon Press are carefully read by a large section of the public. There is a dense wall of ignorance still standing between the average Englishman and the greatest dependency of the Crown; although we can scarcely hope to see it broken down altogether, some of these admirable biographies cannot fail to lower it a little. . . . Mr. Seton-Karr has succeeded in the task, and he has not only presented a large mass of information, but he has brought it together in an attractive form. . . . We strongly recommend the book to all who wish to enlarge the area of their knowledge with reference to India.'—*New York Herald.*

'We have already expressed our sense of the value and timeliness of the series of Indian historical retrospects now issuing, under the editorship of Sir W. W. Hunter, from the Clarendon Press. It is somewhat less than fair to say of Mr. Seton-Karr's monograph upon Cornwallis that it reaches the high standard of literary workmanship which that series has maintained.'—*The Literary World.*

MRS. THACKERAY RITCHIE'S AND MR. RICHARDSON EVANS'

'LORD AMHERST.'

'The story of the Burmese War, its causes and its issues, is re-told with excellent clearness and directness.'—*Saturday Review.*

'Perhaps the brightest volume in the valuable series to which it belongs. . . . The chapter on "The English in India in Lord Amherst's Governor-Generalship" should be studied by those who wish to understand how the country was governed in 1824.'—*Quarterly Review.*

'There are some charming pictures of social life, and the whole book is good reading, and is a record of patience, skill and daring. The public should read it, that it may be chary of destroying what has been so toilsomely and bravely acquired.'—*National Observer.*

'The book will be ranked among the best in the series, both on account of the literary skill shown in its composition and by reason of the exceptional interest of the material to which the authors have had access.'—*St. James's Gazette.*

Opinions of the Press

ON

MR. S. LANE-POOLE'S 'AURANGZÍB.'

'There is no period in Eastern history so full of sensation as the reign of Aurangzíb. ... Mr. Lane-Poole tells this story admirably; indeed, it were difficult to imagine it better told.'—*National Observer.*

'Mr. Lane-Poole writes learnedly, lucidly, and vigorously. ... He draws an extremely vivid picture of Aurangzíb, his strange ascetic character, his intrepid courage, his remorseless overthrow of his kinsmen, his brilliant court, and his disastrous policy; and he describes the gradual decline of the Mogul power from Akbar to Aurangzíb with genuine historical insight.'—*Times.*

'A well-knit and capable sketch of one of the most remarkable, perhaps the most interesting, of the Mogul Emperors.'—*Saturday Review.*

'As a study of the man himself, Mr. Lane-Poole's work is marked by a vigour and originality of thought which give it a very exceptional value among works on the subject.'—*Glasgow Herald.*

'The most popular and most picturesque account that has yet appeared ... a picture of much clearness and force.'—*Globe.*

'A notable sketch, at once scholarly and interesting.'—*English Mail.*

'No one is better qualified than Mr. Stanley Lane-Poole to take up the history and to depict the character of the last of the great Mogul monarchs. ... Aurangzíb's career is ever a fascinating study.'—*Home News.*

'The author gives a description of the famous city of Sháh Jahán, its palaces, and the ceremonies and pageants of which they were the scene. ... Mr. Lane-Poole's well-written monograph presents all the most distinctive features of Aurangzíb's character and career.'—*Morning Post.*

MAJOR ROSS OF BLADENSBURG'S 'MARQUESS OF HASTINGS.'

'Major Ross of Bladensburg treats his subject skilfully and attractively, and his biography of Lord Hastings worthily sustains the high reputation of the Series in which it appears.'—*The Times.*

'This monograph is entitled to rank with the best of the Series, the compiler having dealt capably and even brilliantly with his materials.'—*English Mail.*

'Instinct with interest.'—*Glasgow Evening News.*

'As readable as it is instructive.'—*Globe.*

'A truly admirable monograph.'—*Glasgow Herald.*

'Major Ross has done his work admirably, and bids fair to be one of the best writers the Army of our day has given to the country. ... A most acceptable and entrancing little volume.'—*Daily Chronicle.*

'It is a volume that merits the highest praise. Major Ross of Bladensburg has represented Lord Hastings and his work in India in the right light, faithfully described the country as it was, and in a masterly manner makes one realize how important was the period covered by this volume.'—*Manchester Courier.*

'This excellent monograph ought not to be overlooked by any one who would fully learn the history of British rule in India.'—*Manchester Examiner.*

Opinions of the Press

ON

COLONEL MALLESON'S 'DUPLEIX.'

'In the character of Dupleix there was the element of greatness that contact with India seems to have generated in so many European minds, French as well as English, and a broad capacity for government, which, if suffered to have full play, might have ended in giving the whole of Southern India to France. Even as it was, Colonel Malleson shows how narrowly the prize slipped from French grasp. In 1783 the Treaty of Versailles arrived just in time to save the British power from extinction.'—*Times.*

'One of the best of Sir W. Hunter's interesting and valuable series. Colonel Malleson writes out of the fulness of familiarity, moving with ease over a field which he had long ago surveyed in every nook and corner. To do a small book as well as this on Dupleix has been done, will be recognised by competent judges as no small achievement. When one considers the bulk of the material out of which the little volume has been distilled, one can still better appreciate the labour and dexterity involved in the performance.'—*Academy.*

'A most compact and effective history of the French in India in a little handbook of 180 pages.'—*Nonconformist.*

'Well arranged, lucid and eminently readable, an excellent addition to a most useful series.'—*Record.*

COLONEL MALLESON'S 'AKBAR.'

'Colonel Malleson's interesting monograph on Akbar in the "Rulers of India" (Clarendon Press) should more than satisfy the general reader. Colonel Malleson traces the origin and foundation of the Mughal Empire; and, as an introduction to the history of Muhammadan India, the book leaves nothing to be desired.'—*St. James's Gazette.*

'This volume will, no doubt, be welcomed, even by experts in Indian history, in the light of a new, clear, and terse rendering of an old, but not worn-out theme. It is a worthy and valuable addition to Sir W. Hunter's promising series.'—*Athenæum.*

'Colonel Malleson has broken ground new to the general reader. The story of Akbar is briefly but clearly told, with an account of what he was and what he did, and how he found and how he left India. . . . The native chronicles of the reign are many, and from them it is still possible, as Colonel Malleson has shown, to construct a living portrait of this great and mighty potentate.'—*Scots Observer.*

'The brilliant historian of the Indian Mutiny has been assigned in this volume of the series an important epoch and a strong personality for critical study, and he has admirably fulfilled his task. . . . Alike in dress and style, this volume is a fit companion for its predecessor.'—*Manchester Guardian.*

Opinions of the Press
ON
CAPTAIN TROTTER'S 'WARREN HASTINGS.'

'The publication, recently noticed in this place, of the "Letters, Despatches, and other State Papers preserved in the Foreign Department of the Government of India, 1772-1785," has thrown entirely new light from the most authentic sources on the whole history of Warren Hastings and his government of India. Captain L. J. Trotter's WARREN HASTINGS is accordingly neither inopportune nor devoid of an adequate *raison d'être*. Captain Trotter is well known as a competent and attractive writer on Indian history, and this is not the first time that Warren Hastings has supplied him with a theme.'—*The Times.*

'He has put his best work into this memoir.... His work is of distinct literary merit, and is worthy of a theme than which British history presents none nobler. It is a distinct gain to the British race to be enabled, as it now may, to count the great Governor-General among those heroes for whom it need not blush.'—*Scotsman.*

'Captain Trotter has done his work well, and his volume deserves to stand with that on Dalhousie by Sir William Hunter. Higher praise it would be hard to give it.'—*New York Herald.*

'Captain Trotter has done full justice to the fascinating story of the splendid achievements of a great Englishman.'—*Manchester Guardian.*

'A brief but admirable biography of the first Governor-General of India.'—*Newcastle Chronicle.*

'A book which all must peruse who desire to be "up to date" on the subject.'—*The Globe.*

MR. KEENE'S 'MADHAVA RAO SINDHIA.'

'Mr. Keene has the enormous advantage, not enjoyed by every producer of a book, of knowing intimately the topic he has taken up. He has compressed into these 203 pages an immense amount of information, drawn from the best sources, and presented with much neatness and effect.'—*The Globe.*

'Mr. Keene tells the story with knowledge and impartiality, and also with sufficient graphic power to make it thoroughly readable. The recognition of Sindhia in the "Rulers" series is just and graceful, and it cannot fail to give satisfaction to the educated classes of our Indian fellow-subjects.'—*North British Daily Mail.*

'The volume bears incontestable proofs of the expenditure of considerable research by the author, and sustains the reputation he had already acquired by his "Sketch of the History of Hindustan."'—*Freeman's Journal.*

'Among the eighteen rulers of India included in the scheme of Sir William Hunter only five are natives of India, and of these the great Madhoji Sindhia is, with the exception of Akbar, the most illustrious. Mr. H. G. Keene, a well-known and skilful writer on Indian questions, is fortunate in his subject, for the career of the greatest bearer of the historic name of Sindhia covered the exciting period from the capture of Delhi, the Imperial capital, by the Persian Nadir Shah, to the occupation of the same city by Lord Lake.... Mr. Keene gives a lucid description of his subsequent policy, especially towards the English when he was brought face to face with Warren Hastings.'—*The Daily Graphic.*

Opinions of the Press

ON

MAJOR-GENERAL SIR OWEN BURNE'S
'CLYDE AND STRATHNAIRN.'

'In "Clyde and Strathnairn," a contribution to Sir William Hunter's excellent "Rulers of India" series (Oxford, at the Clarendon Press), Sir Owen Burne gives a lucid sketch of the military history of the Indian Mutiny and its suppression by the two great soldiers who give their names to his book. The space is limited for so large a theme, but Sir Owen Burne skilfully adjusts his treatment to his limits, and rarely violates the conditions of proportion imposed upon him.' . . . 'Sir Owen Burne does not confine himself exclusively to the military narrative. He gives a brief sketch of the rise and progress of the Mutiny, and devotes a chapter to the Reconstruction which followed its suppression.' . . . '—well written, well proportioned, and eminently worthy of the series to which it belongs.'—*The Times.*

'Sir Owen Burne who, by association, experience, and relations with one of these generals, is well qualified for the task, writes with knowledge, perspicuity, and fairness.'—*Saturday Review.*

'As a brief record of a momentous epoch in India this little book is a remarkable piece of clear, concise, and interesting writing.'—*The Colonies and India.*

'Sir Owen Burne has written this book carefully, brightly, and with excellent judgement, and we in India cannot read such a book without feeling that he has powerfully aided the accomplished editor of the series in a truly patriotic enterprise.'—*Bombay Gazette.*

'The volume on "Clyde and Strathnairn" has just appeared, and proves to be a really valuable addition to the series. Considering its size and the extent of ground it covers it is one of the best books about the Indian Mutiny of which we know.'—*Englishman.*

'Sir Owen Burne, who has written the latest volume for Sir William Hunter's "Rulers of India" series, is better qualified than any living person to narrate, from a military standpoint, the story of the suppression of the Indian Mutiny.'—*Daily Telegraph.*

'Sir Owen Burne's book on "Clyde and Strathnairn" is worthy to rank with the best in the admirable series to which it belongs.'—*Manchester Examiner.*

'The book is admirably written; and there is probably no better sketch, equally brief, of the stirring events with which it deals.' —*Scotsman.*

'Sir Owen Burne, from the part he played in the Indian Mutiny, and from his long connexion with the Government of India, and from the fact that he was military secretary of Lord Strathnairn both in India and in Ireland, is well qualified for the task which he has undertaken.'— *The Athenæum.*

Opinions of the Press

ON

VISCOUNT HARDINGE'S 'LORD HARDINGE.'

'An exception to the rule that biographies ought not to be entrusted to near relatives. Lord Hardinge, a scholar and an artist, has given us an accurate record of his father's long and distinguished services. There is no filial exaggeration. The author has dealt with some controversial matters with skill, and has managed to combine truth with tact and regard for the feelings of others.'—*The Saturday Review.*

'This interesting life reveals the first Lord Hardinge as a brave, just, able man, the very soul of honour, admired and trusted equally by friends and political opponents. The biographer . . . has produced a most engaging volume, which is enriched by many private and official documents that have not before seen the light.'—*The Anti-Jacobin.*

'Lord Hardinge has accomplished a grateful, no doubt, but, from the abundance of material and delicacy of certain matters, a very difficult task in a workmanlike manner, marked by restraint and lucidity.'—*The Pall Mall Gazette.*

'His son and biographer has done his work with a true appreciation of proportion, and has added substantially to our knowledge of the Sutlej Campaign.'—*Vanity Fair.*

'The present Lord Hardinge is in some respects exceptionally well qualified to tell the tale of the eventful four years of his father's Governor-Generalship.'—*The Times.*

'It contains a full account of everything of importance in Lord Hardinge's military and political career; it is arranged . . . so as to bring into special prominence his government of India; and it gives a lifelike and striking picture of the man.'—*Academy.*

'The style is clear, the treatment dispassionate, and the total result a manual which does credit to the interesting series in which it figures.'—*The Globe.*

'The concise and vivid account which the son has given of his father's career will interest many readers.'—*The Morning Post.*

'Eminently readable for everybody. The history is given succinctly, and the unpublished letters quoted are of real value.'—*The Colonies and India.*

'Compiled from public documents, family papers, and letters, this brief biography gives the reader a clear idea of what Hardinge was, both as a soldier and as an administrator.'—*The Manchester Examiner.*

'An admirable sketch.'—*The New York Herald.*

'The Memoir is well and concisely written, and is accompanied by an excellent likeness after the portrait by Sir Francis Grant.'—*The Queen.*

Opinions of the Press
ON
SIR HENRY CUNNINGHAM'S 'EARL CANNING.'

'Sir Henry Cunningham's rare literary skill and his knowledge of Indian life and affairs are not now displayed for the first time, and he has enjoyed exceptional advantages in dealing with his present subject. Lord Granville, Canning's contemporary at school and colleague in public life and one of his oldest friends, furnished his biographer with notes of his recollections of the early life of his friend. Sir Henry Cunningham has also been allowed access to the Diary of Canning's private secretary, to the Journal of his military secretary, and to an interesting correspondence between the Governor-General and his great lieutenant, Lord Lawrence.'—*The Times*.

'Sir H. S. Cunningham has succeeded in writing the history of a critical period in so fair and dispassionate a manner as to make it almost a matter of astonishment that the motives which he has so clearly grasped should ever have been misinterpreted, and the results which he indicates so grossly misjudged. Nor is the excellence of his work less conspicuous from the literary than from the political and historical point of view.'—*Glasgow Herald*.

'Sir H. S. Cunningham has treated his subject adequately. In vivid language he paints his word-pictures, and with calm judicial analysis he also proves himself an able critic of the actualities, causes, and results of the outbreak, also a temperate, just appreciator of the character and policy of Earl Canning.'—*The Court Journal*.

REV. W. H. HUTTON'S 'MARQUESS WELLESLEY.'

'Mr. Hutton has brought to his task an open mind, a trained historical judgement, and a diligent study of a great body of original material. Hence he is enabled to present a true, authentic, and original portrait of one of the greatest of Anglo-Indian statesmen, doing full justice to his military policy and achievements, and also to his statesmanlike efforts for the organization and consolidation of that Empire which he did so much to sustain.'—*Times*.

'To the admirable candour and discrimination which characterize Mr. Hutton's monograph as an historical study must be added the literary qualities which distinguish it and make it one of the most readable volumes of the series. The style is vigorous and picturesque, and the arrangement of details artistic in its just regard for proportion and perspective. In short, there is no point of view from which the work deserves anything but praise.'—*Glasgow Herald*.

'The Rev. W. H. Hutton has done his work well, and achieves with force and lucidity the task he sets himself: to show how, under Wellesley, the Indian company developed and ultimately became the supreme power in India. To our thinking his estimate of this great statesman is most just.'—*Black and White*.

'Mr. Hutton has told the story of Lord Wellesley's life in an admirable manner, and has provided a most readable book.'—*Manchester Examiner*.

'Mr. Hutton's range of information is wide, his division of subjects appropriate, and his diction scholarly and precise.'—*Saturday Review*.

Opinions of the Press

ON

SIR LEPEL GRIFFIN'S 'RANJIT SINGH.'

'We can thoroughly praise Sir Lepel Griffin's work as an accurate and appreciative account of the beginnings and growth of the Sikh religion and of the temporal power founded upon it by a strong and remorseless chieftain.'—*The Times.*

'Sir Lepel Griffin treats his topic with thorough mastery, and his account of the famous Mahárájá and his times is, consequently, one of the most valuable as well as interesting volumes of the series of which it forms a part.'—*The Globe.*

'From first to last it is a model of what such a work should be, and a classic.'—*The St. Stephen's Review.*

'The monograph could not have been entrusted to more capable hands than those of Sir Lepel Griffin, who spent his official life in the Punjaub.'—*The Scotsman.*

'At once the shortest and best history of the rise and fall of the Sikh monarchy.'—*The North British Daily Mail.*

'Not only a biography of the Napoleon of the East, but a luminous picture of his country; the chapter on Sikh Theocracy being a notable example of compact thought.'—*The Liverpool Mercury.*

MR. DEMETRIUS BOULGER'S 'LORD WILLIAM BENTINCK.'

'The "Rulers of India" series has received a valuable addition in the biography of the late Lord William Bentinck. The subject of this interesting memoir was a soldier as well as a statesman. He was mainly instrumental in bringing about the adoption of the overland route and in convincing the people of India that a main factor in English policy was a disinterested desire for their welfare. Lord William's despatches and minutes, several of which are textually reproduced in Mr. Boulger's praiseworthy little book, display considerable literary skill and are one and all State papers of signal worth.'—*Daily Telegraph.*

'Mr. Boulger is no novice in dealing with Oriental history and Oriental affairs, and in the career of Lord William Bentinck he has found a theme very much to his taste, which he treats with adequate knowledge and literary skill.'—*The Times.*

'Mr. Boulger writes clearly and well, and his volume finds an accepted place in the very useful and informing series which Sir William Wilson Hunter is editing so ably.'—*Independent.*

Opinions of the Press

ON

MR. J. S. COTTON'S 'MOUNTSTUART ELPHINSTONE.'

'Sir William Hunter, the editor of the series to which this book belongs, was happily inspired when he entrusted the Life of Elphinstone, one of the most scholarly of Indian rulers, to Mr. Cotton, who, himself a scholar of merit and repute, is brought by the nature of his daily avocations into close and constant relations with scholars.... We live in an age in which none but specialists can afford to give more time to the memoirs of even the most distinguished Anglo-Indians than will be occupied by reading Mr. Cotton's two hundred pages. He has performed his task with great skill and good sense. This is just the kind of Life of himself which the wise, kindly, high-souled man, who is the subject of it, would read with pleasure in the Elysian Fields.'—Sir M. E. Grant Duff, in *The Academy*.

'To so inspiring a theme few writers are better qualified to do ample justice than the author of "The Decennial Statement of the Moral and Material Progress and Condition of India." Sir T. Colebrooke's larger biography of Elphinstone appeals mainly to Indian specialists, but Mr. Cotton's slighter sketch is admirably adapted to satisfy the growing demand for a knowledge of Indian history and of the personalities of Anglo-Indian statesmen which Sir William Hunter has done so much to create.'—*The Times*.

DR. BRADSHAW'S 'SIR THOMAS MUNRO.'

'A most valuable, compact and interesting memoir for those looking forward to or engaged in the work of Indian administration.'—*Scotsman*.

'It is a careful and sympathetic survey of a life which should always serve as an example to the Indian soldier and civilian.'—*Yorkshire Post*.

'A true and vivid record of Munro's life-work in almost autobiographical form.'—*Glasgow Herald*.

'Of the work before us we have nothing but praise. The story of Munro's career in India is in itself of exceptional interest and importance.'—*Freeman's Journal*.

'The work could not have been better done; it is a monument of painstaking care, exhaustive research, and nice discrimination.'—*People*.

'This excellent and spirited little monograph catches the salient points of Munro's career, and supplies some most valuable quotations from his writings and papers.'—*Manchester Guardian*.

'It would be impossible to imagine a more attractive and at the same time instructive book about India.'—*Liverpool Courier*.

'It is one of the best volumes of this excellent series.'—*Imperial and Asiatic Quarterly Review*.

'The book throughout is arranged in an admirably clear manner and there is evident on every page a desire for truth, and nothing but the truth.'—*Commerce*.

'A clear and scholarly piece of work.'—*Indian Journal of Education*.

Opinions of the Press

ON

MR. MORSE STEPHENS' 'ALBUQUERQUE.'

'Mr. Stephens' able and instructive monograph . . . We may commend Mr. Morse Stephens' volume, both as an adequate summary of an important period in the history of the relations between Asia and Europe, and as a suggestive treatment of the problem of why Portugal failed and England succeeded in founding an Indian Empire.'—*The Times.*

'Mr. H. Morse Stephens has made a very readable book out of the foundation of the Portuguese power in India. According to the practice of the series to which it belongs it is called a life of Affonso de Albuquerque, but the Governor is only the central and most important figure in a brief history of the Portuguese in the East down to the time when the Dutch and English intruded on their preserves . . . A pleasantly-written and trustworthy book on an interesting man and time.'—*The Saturday Review.*

'Mr. Morse Stephens' *Albuquerque* is a solid piece of work, well put together, and full of interest.'—*The Athenæum.*

'Mr. Morse Stephens' studies in Indian and Portuguese history have thoroughly well qualified him for approaching the subject . . . He has presented the facts of Albuquerque's career, and sketched the events marking the rule of his predecessor Almeida, and of his immediate successors in the Governorship and Viceroyalty of India in a compact, lucid, and deeply interesting form.'—*The Scotsman.*

SIR CHARLES AITCHISON'S 'LORD LAWRENCE.'

'No man knows the policy, principles, and character of John Lawrence better than Sir Charles Aitchison. The salient features and vital principles of his work as a ruler, first in the Punjab, and afterwards as Viceroy, are set forth with remarkable clearness.'—*Scotsman.*

'A most admirable sketch of the great work done by Sir John Lawrence, who not only ruled India, but saved it.'—*Manchester Examiner.*

'Sir Charles Aitchison's narrative is uniformly marked by directness, order, clearness, and grasp; it throws additional light into certain nooks of Indian affairs; and it leaves upon the mind a very vivid and complete impression of Lord Lawrence's vigorous, resourceful, discerning, and valiant personality.'—*Newcastle Daily Chronicle.*

'Sir Charles knows the Punjab thoroughly, and has made this little book all the more interesting by his account of the Punjab under John Lawrence and his subordinates.'—*Yorkshire Post.*

Opinions of the Press

ON

LEWIN BENTHAM BOWRING'S 'HAIDAR ALÍ AND TIPÚ SULTÁN.'

'Mr. Bowring's portraits are just, and his narrative of the continuous military operations of the period full and accurate.'—*Times.*

'The story has been often written, but never better or more concisely than here, where the father and son are depicted vividly and truthfully "in their habit as they lived." There is not a volume of the whole series which is better done than this, or one which shows greater insight.'—*Daily Chronicle.*

'Mr. Bowring has been well chosen to write this memorable history, because he has had the best means of collecting it, having himself formerly been Chief Commissioner of Mysore. The account of the Mysore war is well done, and Mr. Bowring draws a stirring picture of our determined adversary.'—*Army and Navy Gazette.*

'An excellent example of compression and precision. Many volumes might be written about the long war in Mysore, and we cannot but admire the skill with which Mr. Bowring has condensed the history of the struggle. His book is as terse and concise as a book can be.'—*North British Daily Mail.*

'Mr. Bowring's book is one of the freshest and best of a series most valuable to all interested in the concerns of the British Empire in the East.'—*English Mail.*

'The story of the final capture of Seringapatam is told with skill and graphic power by Mr. Bowring, who throughout the whole work shows himself a most accurate and interesting historian.'—*Perthshire Advertiser.*

COLONEL MALLESON'S 'LORD CLIVE.'

'This book gives a spirited and accurate sketch of a very extraordinary personality.'—*Speaker.*

'Colonel Malleson writes a most interesting account of Clive's great work in India—so interesting that, having begun to read it, one is unwilling to lay it aside until the last page has been reached. The character of Clive as a leader of men, and especially as a cool, intrepid, and resourceful general, is ably described; and at the same time the author never fails to indicate the far-reaching political schemes which inspired the valour of Clive and laid the foundation of our Indian Empire.'—*North British Daily Mail.*

'This monograph is admirably written by one thoroughly acquainted and in love with his subject.'—*Glasgow Herald.*

'No one is better suited than Colonel Malleson to write on Clive, and he has performed his task with distinct success. The whole narrative is, like everything Colonel Malleson writes, clear and full of vigour.'—*Yorkshire Post.*

'Colonel Malleson is reliable and fair, and the especial merit of his book is that it always presents a clear view of the whole of the vast theatre in which Clive gradually produces such an extraordinary change of scene.'—*Newcastle Daily Chronicle.*

Opinions of the Press

ON

CAPT. TROTTER'S 'EARL OF AUCKLAND.'

'A vivid account of the causes, conduct, and consequences of "the costly, fruitless, and unrighteous" Afghan War of 1838.'—*St. James's Gazette.*

'To write such a monograph was a thankless task, but it has been accomplished with entire success by Captain L. J. Trotter. He has dealt calmly and clearly with Lord Auckland's policy, domestic and military, with its financial results, and with the general tendency of Lord Auckland's rule.'—*Yorkshire Post.*

'To this distressing story (of the First Afghan War) Captain Trotter devotes the major portion of his pages. He tells it well and forcibly; but is drawn, perhaps unavoidably, into the discussion of many topics of controversy which, to some readers, may seem to be hardly as yet finally decided. . . . It is only fair to add that two chapters are devoted to "Lord Auckland's Domestic Policy," and to his relations with "The Native States of India".'—*The Times.*

'Captain Trotter's *Earl of Auckland* is a most interesting book, and its excellence as a condensed, yet luminous, history of the first Afghan War deserves warm recognition.' *Scotsman.*

'It points a moral which our Indian Rulers cannot afford to forget so long as they still have Russia and Afghanistan to count with.'—*Glasgow Herald.*

Supplementary Volume: price 3s. 6d.

'JAMES THOMASON,' BY SIR RICHARD TEMPLE.

'Sir R. Temple's book possesses a high value as a dutiful and interesting memorial of a man of lofty ideals, whose exploits were none the less memorable because achieved exclusively in the field of peaceful administration.'—*Times.*

'It is the peculiar distinction of this work that it interests a reader less in the official than in the man himself.'—*Scotsman.*

'This is a most interesting book: to those who know India, and knew the man, it is of unparalleled interest, but no one who has the Imperial instinct which has taught the English to rule subject races "for their own welfare" can fail to be struck by the simple greatness of this character.'—*Pall Mall Gazette.*

'Mr. Thomason was a great Indian statesman. He systematized the revenue system of the North-West Provinces, and improved every branch of the administration. He was remarkable, like many great Indians, for the earnestness of his religious faith, and Sir Richard Temple brings this out in an admirable manner.'—*British Weekly.*

'The book is "a portrait drawn by the hand of affection," of one whose life was "a pattern of how a Christian man ought to live." Special prominence is given to the religious aspects of Mr. Thomason's character, and the result is a very readable biographical sketch.'—*Christian.*

Opinions of the Press

ON

SIR AUCKLAND COLVIN'S 'JOHN RUSSELL COLVIN.'

'The concluding volume of Sir William Hunter's admirable "Rulers of India" series is devoted to a biography of John Russell Colvin. Mr. Colvin, as private secretary to Lord Auckland, the Governor-General during the first Afghan War, and as Lieutenant-Governor of the North-West Provinces during the Mutiny, bore a prominent part in the government of British India at two great crises of its history. His biographer is his son, Sir Auckland Colvin, who does full justice to his father's career and defends him stoutly against certain allegations which have passed into history. . . . It is a valuable and effective contribution to an admirable series. In style and treatment of its subject it is well worthy of its companions.'—*Times.*

'Sir Auckland Colvin has been able to throw new light on many of the acts of Lord Auckland's administration, and on the state of affairs at Agra on the outbreak of the Mutiny. . . . This memoir will serve to recall the splendid work which Colvin really performed in India, and to exhibit him as a thoroughly honourable man and conscientious ruler.'—*Daily Telegraph.*

'This book gives an impressive account of Colvin's public services, his wide grasp of native affairs, and the clean-cut policy which marked his tenure of power.'—*Leeds Mercury.*

'The story of John Colvin's career indicates the lines on which the true history of the first Afghan War and of the Indian Mutiny should be written. . . . Not only has the author been enabled to make use of new and valuable material, but he has also constructed therefrom new and noteworthy explanations of the position of affairs at two turning-points in Indian history.'—*Academy.*

'High as is the standard of excellence attained by the volumes of this series, Sir Auckland Colvin's earnest work has reached the high-water mark.'—*Army and Navy Gazette.*

'Sir Auckland Colvin has done his part with great tact and skill. As an example of the clear-sighted way in which he treats the various Indian problems we may cite what he says on the education of the natives—a question always of great moment to the subject of this biography.'—*Manchester Guardian.*

'Sir Auckland Colvin gives us an admirable study of his subject, both as a man of affairs and as a student in private life. In doing this, his picturesque theme allows him, without outstepping the biographical limits assigned, to present graphic pictures of old Calcutta and Indian life in general.'—*Manchester Courier.*

'This little volume contains pictures of India, past and present, which it would be hard to match for artistic touch and fine feeling. We wish there were more of the same kind to follow.'—*St. James's Gazette.*

'The monograph is a valuable addition to a series of which we have more than once pointed out the utility and the excellence.'—*Glasgow Herald.*

www.ingramcontent.com/pod-product-compliance
Lightning Source LLC
Chambersburg PA
CBHW031752230426
43669CB00007B/582